Invisible

Gayleen Gaeke

INFINITY
PUBLISHING

Copyright © 2012 by Gayleen Gaeke

ISBN 978-0-7414-7433-9

Printed in the United States of America

Published August 2012

INFINITY PUBLISHING
1094 New DeHaven Street, Suite 100
West Conshohocken, PA 19428-2713
Toll-free (877) BUY BOOK
Local Phone (610) 941-9999
Fax (610) 941-9959
Info@buybooksontheweb.com
www.buybooksontheweb.com

THANK YOU

"All that is necessary for the evil to triumph is that good men do nothing."

Edmund Burke

A journey towards wholeness is soothed by the passage of time when good men listen to those things that are hard to hear. Thank you to all who have had the patience and fortitude to create a safe place for me amongst the thorns of my childhood. I owe a debt of gratitude, especially to my husband who bravely watched the night terrors and re-living, who shook me out of my childhood pain and brought me back to adulthood. He is the one who explained over and over the abuse was not my fault; I was not the guilty one. This secret belonged to a Father who was incapable of being anything like a Father, but rather a cruel dictator.

Most of all, to all who took me seriously, listened and prayed for my release, for the freedom to cry again, to stop darkness and fear from abiding, for love to begin anew and to live a life that included an abiding joy. To my friends who believed my story and walked the journey with me, who bonded with me in my cry for wholeness.

Lastly, to Jesus the one who comes ever closer amidst the suffering, showing His love through people. He was and will continue to be a messenger of peace and calmness amidst the storm.

Thank you, thank you to all.

TABLE OF CONTENTS

FOREWORD

The majority of modern societies have agreed for quite some time that child abuse is wrong and have put laws into place to protect that vulnerable segment of society. It has been commonly understood and accepted that children are adversely affected by neglect and abuse. But only recently have studies begun to uncover the profound consequences of this abuse to a child's development and how it continues to affect them into adulthood.

These studies have revealed that abuse damages every part of a child; emotionally, physically, relationally, no aspect of that child is left untouched. In fact, we now believe that childhood abuse has such a horrific effect that it physically alters the structure and chemistry of the child's brain.

In adulthood, abused children often suffer from Post Traumatic Stress Disorder (PTSD), similar to soldiers who have been in live battle situations. This PTSD reveals itself in such things as depression, flashbacks and re-living (memories so intense that the person is actually once again in the abusive situation), intense rage, night terrors and exaggerated reactions.

A natural defense mechanism for such trauma is to bury the memories. For many, these painful memories are buried so deep that they are never dealt with, never diagnosed, never treated. For others, the memories are uncovered through perhaps another traumatic life event or through counselling or just through normal life experiences. No matter how they are brought to the surface, once they are exposed, dealing with them is an agonizing and often scary journey.

I am continually amazed at the courage with which my wife faces her past. It has been a very rough ride, with many setbacks along the way. But through it all, she has continued to push forward. She is learning to share her struggles with trusted sojourners. She is not afraid to talk about her experiences with other abuse victims, often times giving them courage to face their own demons. She does not shy away from the flood of memories, but confronts them, thus reducing their power over her. She may never be completely free from her night terrors, her intense re-living or her bouts of depression; but she is learning to live one day at a time, seeing each day lived as one more day of freedom from her past.

Writing this book was a very difficult undertaking for her. Seeing some memories in black and white often served to dredge up even more from the hidden depths. However, it has been an important step for her. It has served to add legitimacy to the reality of her past abuse. And it continues to be a part of her journey towards healing.

May those who read this book be inspired by her story and take courage to walk into the next step in their own journey.

George Gaeke, B.A., M.A., GISP

INTRODUCTION

I was losing touch with my own life – the daily routine that should have been comforting to me was becoming boring and mundane. It felt all too easy. I couldn't figure out if I was living in some sort of denial or if life was supposed to be slow and plodding. I was invisible.

Invisibility is a powerful force. It creates a shield of self-protection. Just as you are trying to hide from pain in the real life, you hide from people and places. But life didn't allow me to stay invisible forever. Experiences and encounters with others began to expose my soul to the harsh realities of my childhood. A long forgotten cavern, full of pain and darkness, was opened up.

Life has never followed any structure. Confusion has attacked me from every side. It has been an evolution of learning rather than a strict timeline with nicely placed commas and periods. This is how my soul came to, out of a world of abuse. This is how my soul is being healed - stripping away the secrecy. Meandering through these childhood memories has created a new me, a better me.

What is in this book creates pleasure and pain, warmth and devastation. It is both tragic and true. Some of what you read is in story form, some from journaling and some random poetry. It came to me in untamed spurts that resist structure, in a misshapen form. I would write for days and days and then not at all. The harshness of childhood reality was sometimes too hard to face.

I do not mean this book to be an act of self-redemption, nor a voice for the bitterness against my abusers. If anything it has taught me that the exploration of one's childhood is to be treaded on as holy ground.

My longing, rather, is for those who have sat on the edge for so long to come out with their stories, even if it be only to one trusted friend. It took me over thirty long years to stop the denial

3

of my undesirable childhood and to face the truth, the reality of all that had happened. Perhaps, it also took me that long to feel safe and secure enough to acknowledge the reality of abuse. It could be that for the first time in my life I hoped against hope that someone would listen and believe, that there would be a strong hand, and an open heart to trust in. That is what I wish for all those who have experienced secrets in their lives.

A MICROCOSM

"The earth is full of overwhelming suffering; it is also full of conquering."

Mahatma Gandhi

That day was like walking into a war zone. The false, superficial peace that had lain upon the family for generations had disappeared long ago. My sister and I walked into the sky-blue house, giggling and laughing about the events of the day. We were all grown up, or so we thought.

For years now we had been stymied by the events at hand, the changes in our family. Mother's memory was growing ever worse. The thought that she had Alzheimer's had crossed our mind more than once. She rarely moved from her chair. It was a soft, burgundy red and she looked so very tiny in it and often so very tired. Her osteoporosis ran severely along the length of her shrinking spine, leaving her almost dwarfish. She rarely got up for a hello and a hug anymore. The remote control that would move the coveted chair up and down to a more soothing position always lay on the right-hand side of the arm of the chair. It was easily within her reach, ready to lower her down to walk to the door when company came, yet she often remained in the chair. Whether she had grown comfortable with pain or just plain forgot that the device belonged to her, neither my sister nor I knew. All we did know was that the device could make her more comfortable right where she was.

We chatted about the weather and the neighbours. Mother always loved watching the neighbourhood children from her most excellent vantage point. A large picture window became her movie screen as she watched each house for some sign of life.

She almost seemed to know the neighbourhood better than her own home--a can of soup for lunch, the frozen pizza mistakenly left somewhere, anywhere but on her own kitchen counter.

Remembering where her things were in her own house seemed an impossible burden.

She had her own rituals though; she was insistent that she brush her teeth every day. She always jotted the dates and times of appointments down, but she rarely did anything the same way any more. Each day was more and more of a muddled mess, and between Father and Mother, and all of us siblings, we didn't know the outcome of each day.

Would supper be made for five o'clock? Would medication be taken at the right time? Laundry done before clean clothes were needed again?

Still, for the most part it had become enjoyable visiting with her. Only one subject was untouchable, that of Mother's independence. At the age of 76, she was insistent that she never forgot a thing. Great drama ensued upon any mention of her mental incompetence. Gradually, we learnt to leave it all unsaid. The order of the day was a contrived, yet pleasant peace.

Eventually, Father heard the chattering and the slow shuffling of tired feet could be heard in the distance. This sliding sound from stair to stair told us of another occupant who called this house his home. My sister and I relaxed on our respective couches, making no attempt to greet this man in any friendly way.

He was a sight; unkempt, whiskers grown long on his face, hair fallen down over squinty eyes. Layers of greasy hair and dandruff lay on the collar of his worn out red-checkered flannel shirt. His pants were pulled up high, roped together with a pair of stretched out burgundy suspenders. Malnutrition had made it impossible not to live without this made-up hoist. It was yet another invention of his, the gaping, too large waist of his pants acting as a good conductor of air in and around an unwashed body.

He stood, as always, with one hand on the rose-coloured chair that rested next to the entrance door. He had tired himself out just by rising from the depths of his retreat in the dark, cold basement.

Today my sister and I had a little something special up our sleeves. Joy handed my parents the ever-precious bubble packs filled with tiny, candy-coloured medication. Mother opened the end table beside her massaging chair and put the packs in an old shiny Christmas bag while Father whisked his goodies off back down the hallway, like a Grinch hoarding his take.

Upon the Grinch's return, the usual conversation resumed. The yard, the street, the neighbours, the small nondescript town all gave them an unwarranted sense of security, of safety, of welfare.

Keith had been summoned by his sisters to try to settle the problems that came with Mother and Father living together. What we saw as a special journey gave him acid indigestion. He grimaced as he drove up the driveway. He despised these days. Trying to convince his parents to move into a care home was like trying to take a cat for a walk. But today he won the draw as he whisked Mother off to the restaurant. Rambling with Mother was a far easier task than the one cast to my sister and me.

My Father needed his meals made and his pillows fluffed and his wife was the only one who knew how to do it right. If she could not take care of him, who would?

It had come to this standoff many times. The four of us sitting in the living room with its bright red carpet, discussing the crucial changes that needed to take place. It seemed easy for Father to forget the most recent of events. His wife falling down to the living room floor, lying on the floor for hours. Father calling the police in a panic, then his son and then eventually the ambulance being called. Never thinking of a neighbour or someone close by to help him. Mother was hospitalized for days while Father put in many calls to his children as to when she would come home. It was hard to tell whether his imploring was over Mother's health or over the unrelenting fact that he had no meals to eat. The two of us daughters put all we could into reminding Father of this, wanting to push him towards moving away from his little blue house towards some real safety.

But he was not about to be pushed around by his daughters; first the whimpering over the present situation set in. Apparently we had no clue how difficult life was for him. Mother was throwing things away. She abused him. She was not nice and now we were mean and cruel to him too. The derision in his voice grew stronger. He was incensed that we had no compassion for him. My sister would not back down. From her vantage point as a nurse, Mother needed to move to a care home to get the help she needed. She left Father with many questions, none of which he liked, or was willing to accept. Moving was not on the top of his list and he made that abundantly clear. I sat on the couch staring into space. This was an age-old battle. I saw no one winning; it was only a loss for everyone. Pretending all was well in my own little world proved disastrous. By now, Joy was up and yelling, "You bastard, think of someone other than yourself for once. When will you ever grow up?"

Father whimpered, "Don't talk to me like that; I'm your Father."

"Then do something for your wife. She will die, starving to death because she can't remember to eat, sitting in her own urine. Do you want that?"

"Don't yell at me." A pout spread across Father's face. "I don't know what to do when you yell at me like that," he said again. Father, at the age of 78, shuffled up to my sister and in his most pitiful tone cried, "I just want you to love me, please love me."

Things were no different now at the ages of 47 and 50 than at the ages of 10 and 13. Father was still making the same threats, his demands growing louder and louder.

Just like that Joy flew off the couch, running down the hallway in a powerful rage. The language on her tongue worsened with each moment, until she cracked under her own bitterness. Before she could hold the words in they passed her twisted lips, "I have always hated you."

Father was scraping along behind, but did not even seem to notice the force of the spite in Joy's tone.

I was growing concerned, and so I came slowly along behind the two. I peeked around the corner. The vision that came to bear down on me was too much to watch. Father had Joy by the shoulders and he was shaking her. But the words coming out of his mouth caused such an intense feeling in me, one that I had learnt to deny long ago.

"I'm going to kill you," he said.

Said not once, but twice, with greater malice and an even greater cause for worry the second time.

I scrunched down onto the floor and tried to think of what to do, scream, run in terror, push Father away. But before I could finish at least one complete thought I felt my sister bolt past this monster and race into the living room. She sat shaking on the couch and I sat staring at her.

The background noise held an awful wailing, "I just want you to love me, just love me."

I looked at my sister and with my eyes, told her not to move. She would be safe as long as I was in the room. I proclaimed loud enough for this monster to hear, "You are safe with me in the room; you don't have to speak to him ever again." It was like we had just stepped back in time. Except one important thing had changed. We were there for each other. The scathing remarks, the torrid looks had changed to a blankness. This time as we looked into each other's eyes, we knew there was a lot of our childhood we needed to face but there was contentment just the same. After all, we stood together.

The stress and strain of Fathers' harsh words and the rare happiness of good times were still with me, even after the many years of having grown up and been away from home. Thinking back to my childhood, a strange knot grew in my stomach. For me, the longing of ever being loved with parental love was too precarious to think about.

PUZZLING

"It is easier for a Father to have children than for children to have a real Father."

Pope John XXII

As a child, Father's influence on my life left me feeling all alone and, I have to admit, that if I wanted anyone's love in the family, it was his. The problem was catching it. It was like trying to hold onto a slippery fish. Just when you thought you had it, it wriggled free, right out of your hands and back into the water. Starting all over was no easy task; you had to find the right lure, attach it to the rod and hurl it through the air at the right speed and in the exact direction he had gone off in. Most of the time was spent sitting and waiting for that same old grey fish to latch onto the lure again. Something inside me was resigned to the game and something relished in it. After all, I actually might succeed one day and win the glory of a handsome fish upon my rod. Really though, there was no sense in hoping for one minute that he cherished me, for the next minute, his attentions would turn away.

My journey through daughterhood proved no different. One minute Father cherished me, the next minute his attentions turned away. Most of my relationship with Father was based on how well I performed. If I obeyed him, I was hailed as a princess. If I failed to live up to his impeccable standards, his words were taunting and cruel. The foundations of my small life were shaken.

This constant pressure to perform was exhausting, and for some reason I never developed the same cocoon of protection as I did with Mother. The desire to be loved by this rigid, rule-ridden man was too strong to overcome. I allowed vulnerability in; I waited for kindness to show itself. Just one word of approval would have brought joy to my empty heart. The teeter-totter of acceptance was wobbly, veering out of control. One moment I was happy for what little relationship with Father I had, his image held high. The next moment I pitied myself for my instinctual longing for love from a selfish, aloof man.

Mother cherished her position as the protector of the small flock she had borne. Mostly, she attempted to bring us relief from Father's wrath. It seemed that whenever Father rushed madly in the door with one authoritative command or another, she knew about it before he had hardly opened the door. It was as though she had a sixth sense about these things. Later on I was to learn that she had the perfect vantage view from the kitchen table. She would scurry about as though a great emergency was about to take place and it usually did. A tractor part needed to be special ordered from John Deere immediately. The half ton had mired itself down into the slick, black clay of Manitoba's landscape. The milk thistles with their deep purple flowers had grown tall in the struggling barley field. And Mother was ever there to meet the constant crises.

She protected us from Father's wrath as best as she knew how. She was the only one who could discern Father's wishes. She relayed his every wish to her children and we complied with great trepidation. I did not envy her role.

Although she tirelessly protected us from Father, she did nothing to keep me, in particular, from her own wrath. I lived in the shadow of her relentless anger. I could do nothing to appease her. The blue-tiled bathroom was never shiny enough. The green Corelle dish set was never scraped properly after a particularly greasy meal. And I certainly never moved quickly enough for her taste. I always faltered, never living up to the challenge of Mother's expectations either.

I could tell by the look on her face that she was concerned about my introverted nature but she never commented on it. I cannot say I was unthankful for that.

HEAD OVER HEELS

The school bus sped away, down the big road leaving a wake of dust behind. Andy and I sauntered towards the house, knowing we would be kicked out of the house after school. Mother said we were too loud and rambunctious for her. She preferred to live the solitary life away from the noise of children. Her life appeared to be a lonely one. When you live all by yourself, life becomes mundane and boring. I could not understand my Mother on this point.

I wanted very much to have one good friend. At home, that friend was my younger brother. Andy and I were pushed together by circumstance but grew to love each other just the same. We remained friends in a stranger's world.

With the bang of the front door, Mother had kicked us out again. We competed to see who could get to their bike first. Then we rode as fast as we could down the main farm driveway. We swerved severely to the left, down into the weed-ridden ditch, defining our award-winning landing on the other side by whether we remained upright, but mostly we just crashed with a thud, unable to save ourselves from going head first over the front of our bikes.

Diving into the underbrush, we pretended an army of soldiers was attacking us. Our imaginations became our guide. We lay there in the grasses, laughing and rolling over onto the twigs and rotting leaves, our sides heaving. Then standing up one more time we found branches, pretending they were our weaponry. We ran a most amazing race, trying to beat each other through the dense underbrush, shooting at our torturers as we went. Bam-bam, and again, soon they were all conquered by our awkward artillery.

Looking towards that old driveway we pushed our bikes through the woods down the ditch and up onto it. "On your mark, get set, go," our voices rang through the air. Getting our second wind, we leapt onto our battered bikes and rode as fast as we could all the way down the driveway, did an abrupt U-turn at the end of it and glared at the road before us. Dust lay in the air. I took one long look into Andy's face, daring him on, and then launched my bike forward with a huge wheelie. Pushing as hard as we could on the rusty pedals, our speed grew exponentially. The ditch was coming closer and closer. Then with all the courage we possessed we willed our land machines up into the sky and over the ditch at a crazy speed. Flying along in wild abandon, the exhilaration running high, our screams of delight were loud enough to be heard throughout the land. We landed with a sound thud on the other side, ending up in a crumpled heap, lying on the forest floor laughing even harder than before. After all, we had conquered our enemy, the farmyard ditch. There was room for celebration.

This time as we manpowered our bikes up the ditch it wasn't the dip we would conquer. The end of the driveway meant a sharp rise and the beginning of the big road. This was a dream that came ever closer. This time, with all the courage we possessed we threw our dilapidated bikes up the rise in the road and into the air at a wild speed. Flying through the air, the exhilaration running high, our screams ringing through the air, we landed and put the brakes on by standing high on the pedals of our bikes and pushing our feet backwards. The dust flew and a satisfying scrape could be heard on the road. We turned to each other. We had dared disobedience by driving on the big road but the front bike spokes had just passed the squeaky clean test, being just at the end of our driveway but not on the big road. We had remained as close to Mother's rules as possible, a shot of adrenaline sent a major thrill through our child bodies. Laughing even harder than before, we turned around and drove the long journey home for supper just in time.

I can still hear our laughter as we did or tried to do jumps with our bikes through the row of trees surrounding the old farmyard. Although we mostly fell headfirst over the front of the bike, diving into the underbrush, a barrage of enemy soldiers attacking us, we never tired of it. To us it wasn't boring repetition. There was meaning behind it. It was a moment of true happiness.

Andy and I did a lot together. He was my younger brother by two years. He was already a prankster before he even learnt how to walk. The glint of a smile on his face proved that. He crossed many lines with Mother that the rest of us would never even think of crossing. His cute little dimples were just charming enough to melt her anger away.

Peanut butter and honey were his closest friends. He wore the sticky brown paste on his face, on his shirt; he even spread it on the table in his mad haste to consume yet another sandwich. He would have taken it to bed with him if Mother would have let him.

Andy and I played together outside a lot. It was easy being around him. We were friends, laughing and dreaming with one another. We helped each other take the gloom out of a rainy day.

We built boats in the machine shed. They resembled a couple of 2x4s nailed together in various fashions. We attached strings to nails pounded into the front of the boat. We sailed them in the ditch and little ponds of water we found around the yard.

We skipped stones on the pond, stealing gravel off the driveway. This was not a winner with Father!

We slid down the pig barn roof on our bright blue crazy carpets in the dead of winter. It was a long, snowy run that brought freezing tears to our eyes and warmth to our hearts.

Skating on the man-made pond was a chore. Cleaning off the sparkling white snow with a big awkward shovel took forever. Putting on our second-hand skates as tightly as we could, we would bump along the rough ice. The sun shone brightly glaring in our eyes. Our eyelashes stuck together from our watering eyes and frosty breath. Breaking the rules by taking off all of our winter headgear was a welcome relief. Andy and I laughed aloud. Sometimes life was good. Days like these were a welcome relief from our stern and joyless home life.

DAYS OF INNOCENCE

This sense of kinship with my younger brother developed because, for a long while, I was left behind while my brother and sister got to go to school. It was about two miles away from the old farmyard and a big yellow school bus came and picked up Keith and Joy. They somberly walked all the way down the long gravel driveway. There was no racing or playing. Their lunch kits swayed back and forth in their hands and sometimes they swirled them around in a complete 360. They sloughed along, in a trance-like state, not giving their surroundings any consideration.

Although I never really got along all that well with my older siblings, their presence meant that I would go unnoticed by Mother and Father. Now I was recognized as a part of the family and as such, had responsibilities. While my Mother was busy with household tasks such as laundry, baking bread, and cleaning I was to keep my younger brother busy and out of the way.

We played games galore, building with wooden blocks of different colours, making puzzles, playing dress-up. Andy always let me dress him up in a skirt and pearls...and sometimes I would even get Mother's lipstick on him. He didn't seem to mind at all. But Mother did mind and she ruined my inspired attempts to make my brother into my sister.

We made tents out of blankets and ski poles and had afternoon naps in them. Most of the sleep time was spent opening and closing our eyes to see if our partner was awake. I am sure this venture took no longer than five minutes. Then we whooped and hollered at each other, going round and round the tent in circles, pretending we were Indians. Feathers we had found outside next to the chicken coop were placed behind our ears. This added just the right amount of authenticity needed to create the special effects.

We watched Sesame Street, trying to waddle like Big Bird; and Mr. Dress-Up; even the Friendly Giant, Rusty Rooster and the kindly Giraffe. We played pirates outside (Mother would not allow that game inside, for what reason I do not know) and proclaimed such sentiments as, "Hardee har, Mate."

We always kept the best game for the last hurrah, Hide and Seek. Although there were only two of us, we added our nearest and dearest stuffed animals into the mix as a part of the hunt. We took turns hiding our small participants in the bushes, trees, the flowerbeds, even in the old red barn. We wandered around, trying to find the dusty dolls and bears. In the end we lay flat on our backs in the grass, laughing like there was no tomorrow. It was impossible to find our favourite toys spread out on at least an acre. Instead we skipped around in the bright sunshine holding hands and working together to find them. We were no longer competing against each other, although I grumbled a bit to see my favourite doll dusty and dirty. I stuck out my tongue at my younger brother and told him I didn't see how he could be trusted to play this game if he couldn't take proper care of my babies.

SONGS OF SPRING

Andy and I always found time to play together, even in the rain. One crisp morning we made our way outside, despite a drizzle that would have kept most of our playmates inside.

We jumped into our raincoats so we wouldn't catch a chill. Actually, truth be told, we would never have worn them if Mother hadn't been around. T-shirts and hoodies were enough for us. The boots and the jackets were both ten times too big on us as they were hand-me-downs.

We wandered around the yard trying to find big plastic buckets; finally, we found old fertilizer buckets from the last spring's seeding, empty and waiting for us, daring us on. Finding them here and there, we were happy for the thrill of the hunt. Finally, we had two of the biggest and we stomped down the lane and up to the big road. We were not allowed on the big road without permission, but that did not bother us today. We did not intend to break that rule. We climbed down the steep ditch, watching a little river of water flowing smoothly along.

We ran to the row of bushes, which marked our yard and started breaking off branches. Finally we retrieved the biggest and the best and ran back to take our mark. Taking the long stick, we began to measure the depth of the water. This was no easy task because we had to bend as far across the ditch as we could and slowly put the stick straight up and down in the water. We would pull it out, coming close to an ill-fated doom as we wobbled back and forth on our rubber boot heels in the muck. We would come dangerously close to falling in. Andy did the measuring, not because he was the bravest but because he had it down to a precise art. For the final test, we would see if the water would be so high that it would fill our boots if we were to venture into the murky water. Today we made it by about two inches. We grinned widely at each other slapping our hands together in a high five. The sun had come out and everything was going our way.

Grabbing our buckets, we ventured back into the ditch. We could hear the croaking and singing of the small green, slimy creatures and our excitement grew. Filling our buckets with some water, we made sure there was just the right amount settled on the bottom. I hoped that the dirt would settle down so we could see our wonders of creation. The rocks would come later. They would be the perches for these fine specimens of frogs. We worked with speed and agility. After all, this was one of our favourite springtime activities. It was still chilly and our hands grew stiff and red. At first I tried to wear my small thin gloves from the dollar store, but the frigid water soaked right through them and only made matters worse.

As the frogs sang their first songs of spring, we caught them one by one and put them in their new home. The feel of their skin was delightful as they tried their hardest to slither out and return to their natural habitat. They wanted to be free. The sloshing water in our boots went unfelt as we worked feverishly to catch them, big and small, green and greener.

On and on we went until it was time to carry the heavy buckets to their final resting place. We carried them back to the yard and started working on a new home for our long-legged pets. We gathered rocks and anything we thought they might eat, mostly grass. We really hadn't the faintest clue what to feed them. When their new environment was complete, we squatted down beside the buckets and watched.

The frogs swam and dived and we believed they were happy in their home away from home. Their slippery skin glinted in the sun. Their spots stood out, adding character to their tiny bodies. I smiled down on them maternally, naming each of them in my mind. There was Greenie and Spot, Leaper, Croaker..., and the list went on.

Our hard work had paid off. We put the pails in a safe place, usually by the old red granary and half covered them over with lids so predators couldn't get in. Little did we know the ill fate that awaited those frogs. All we cared about was that we had done the right thing by saving them from the ravages of nature. They would be safe in their new manmade pond. With more high fives, we were off onto the next venture. All was well with the world.

Hearing Mother's voice calling us for lunch stopped us dead in our tracks. We knew we had better race along to the house or else. Reluctantly we went to our spots at the kitchen table. After lunch, we returned triumphantly to our play, stomachs full and ready for more fun and frivolity.

We often went exploring, looking for objects of curiosity and intrigue. These treasures included eagle feathers, and chicken feathers too, pretty stones, and bright yellow and red leaves in the fall, gnarly sticks, and oh, so many other prizes. We collected them all in an old ice cream bucket and returned each day to see if the treasures still held their magical powers. Nature had its way of making us forget the harsh reality of life on the farm.

When we were done with our adventures for the day, we would race around the Caragana bush. It was long and became a Grand Prix racetrack. Sometimes we would start out on one end of it and see who would beat who to the far end. Other times, we would race around and around trying to catch each other. Mostly we just laughed at each other, tripping over gangly feet that had become much too big for our bodies.

When we were near to exhausted, we started picking the small, freshly budded, yellow flowers off the bush. When we each had our own handful, we would sit down in the grass and eat them one by one. The tiny buds were sweet. They tasted like honey and smelled heavenly. Sometimes I wondered if they were any good for me but they never made us sick so I figured it was OK.

These were happy times just between my brother, Andy and myself.

There was always some lively story happening in our innocent imaginations. Nothing held us back from being friends in those days. Our world was prime time news, with never a dull moment.

UTTER ABANDONMENT

How I long to be that little girl again, the one who could laugh while running in the gardens and grass as if there were no tomorrow. She twirled this way and that through a garden of dandelions in utter abandonment. Bare feet were a necessity. The little girl carefully dropped down to her knees intent on picking each brightly coloured yellow flower. The sticky milk from the flowers dripping slowly onto her tiny hands felt soft and warm. Oh, so pleased with the beauty that lay in her hands she skipped up towards the farmhouse door. She twisted the nob as quietly as she could and cringed when the door let out a squeak. Leaving it open so the surprise would not be spoiled she slowly peaked her head around the corner of the hallway and into the kitchen.

She found exactly what she was looking for. Mother was sitting at the kitchen table reading a favourite book. She raised her eyes up above the pages with a slight smile on her face. The happy girl brought the yellow "posies" around from behind my back to greet her head on. Our eyes met, sparkling together, a connection with no words spoken.

Mother jumped up from her chair, humming now and grabbed her favourite vase from the kitchen cupboard. I offered her the flowers with the simplicity that only a child can. She gracefully took the offering with a little bow and planted the blossoms in the middle of a vase full of water. She took me up on her lap and the two of us stared happily at the fruits of my labour.

DOLLS AND ME

When I was little, I loved to play with dolls. My favourite was my Baby Tender Love™. I got her for Christmas one year and quickly became entranced with her. She was soft and had a little belly and even a belly button. Her legs and arms bent this way and that. Her hair was flaxen, short and curly. There wasn't much I could do with it except put barrettes on either side.

She had her own little bottle that you could fill up with water. I made diapers out of old cloth napkins from Mother's supply. Then I would hold her close in my arms and feed her as if she was real. Her diaper slowly got wet and I used to chide her as I changed her diaper yet another time. The clothes she came with were bright, yellow and frilly. They were very pretty.

Come to think of it, when I was playing with her, I became a different child. I grew a softer side, becoming gentle and a little more compassionate. There was never anyone around so nobody saw this side of me. I have to say, as a child, that I was quite unaware of it. I found nothing unusual about loving my dolls to death and turning around and jabbing my little brother in the ribs. These lifeless creatures brought out the best in me. I had several more dolls, but like most of the ones from the '70s, they were stiff-bodied, coarse-haired, permanently smiling playthings.

I made clothes for all of them out of old scraps Mother gave me. The fabric was multi-coloured and shaped, well, like a scrap. I made my own patterns for them out of big brown bags and cut crudely down a pencil line created especially for the doll dress. Then the painstaking job of sewing started. Threading the needle was always a challenge and sewing in a straight line even more so. Sometimes I snuck downstairs and used Mother's sewing machine. It was a constant struggle to get the thread through the needle and half the time it came out as I started to sew. Once I got going, things really took off. The lines were straighter and I had fun zooming along. I was in my glory as I dreamt of what a true princess my doll would look like in her new apparel.

If the cloth was extra wrinkly, I would take the time to iron the new creation. Otherwise, I would start dressing my doll, hoping with all my might the new item would fit. I usually had to make a few alterations just so the dress would even fit over her head. Ahhhh, such was the life of a seamstress. So much work was demanded in order to obtain true perfection. When the dress was done, we waltzed around my tiny bedroom doing the dance of joy. My Baby Tender Love™ was more beautiful than ever and I loved her with all my heart.

This love for dolls was not over when I started to get older, for I had Barbie™ dolls too. Making outfits for them was a little more difficult. My fingers were poked repeatedly. Usually my designer creations didn't fit and I would have to start all over from scratch. My crooked pencil lines grew wider, then thinner with each mark and I could never follow exactly where they went. Once I tried to make a shiny pink dress out of slippery material. The edges of the fabric were so jagged and misshapen that there was no telling where to sew a straight line. I laughed to myself and once again, thought, "Ahh, the life of a seamstress!"

GOLDEN RULE DAYS

A five-year-old does not think so much about the passage of time, but that does not stop time from passing. Those days of reckless abandon with my brother lasted a long time, but hardly long enough. Soon the time for school began.

I can still remember my first day of school clearly. I was dressed in a homemade outfit made from the ever-present, eternal Fortrel fabric Mother found in the store. She searched down deep in the bargain bin at the back of the fabric store, finding a never-ending supply of treasures. Bringing her finds home she would cut clothes from patterns she saved year after year. She would make them bigger or smaller depending on the child, until the pattern was all ripped and crumpled around the edges. Her beige Singer™ sewing machine was her pride and joy. She was an expert seamstress, using all of her efforts to create 1960s fashion with a twist. Economics came first. It was always the cheapest and the brightest fabric. Mother's motivation was for us to look the best possible for the least possible. I have to say she succeeded almost every time.

I felt proud in my new duds but the fear and excitement of going to school for the first time was growing strong in me. I stepped out onto the porch to face the new day. The gravel driveway I walked down seemed very long but, with one step in front of the other, I eventually made it to the end of the driveway. I stirred up the dust with my shoes by sliding this way and that. I had finally made it and there I was standing next to my brother and sister. It was kind of windy and cold. Most of the crops were in the bins so the wind blew dirt from the fields across the prairie.

Keith threw rocks in the ditch. He tried to find the flat ones to skip them into the water but honestly, he wasn't very good at it. My sister, well, she just stood there swaying back and forth, anticipating her next year of school. We could see the bus a half mile down the road roaring towards us, dust kicking up behind. It looked like the driver was moving at a mad pace. He picked up our neighbours first. They lived a little way down the road and we could see them getting on the bus. They were all veterans so they knew how this thing went. My whole body was shaking as I watched the big yellow bus door close after the last of the neighbours where on. This meant that we were next. I bent down and picked up my things from off the driveway. The rocks stopped flying from my brother's hand and he picked up his knapsack and lunch kit. He stood at the front of an imaginary line and acted as if he was the leader of our small gang. I fell in line at the end with my bright new orange lunch kit held firmly in my hand. I was so proud of it because it had decals on it from cereal boxes.

Our bus driver was militant, sitting straight and tall and opening the door of the bus with exact motions. It was the usual yellow bus. The driver was so good he could stop in almost the exact same place each day of the week.

As I climbed the monstrous steps (there were three), I remembered that Keith and Joy had made it abundantly clear that I was not to sit near them on the bus. Keith sauntered to the back, Joy to the center and I sat right smack dab in the front, feet together, lunch kit centered perfectly on my lap.

I wasn't surprised that Keith wanted no association with me for he was five years my senior and made sure I knew about it. He was constantly playing pranks on me. I grew to expect this behaviour as a normal part of life.

I cannot say that I envied his position in the family. He worked hard to obey Father's every command. His list of work was unending. I don't know how many times he went back to repeat the same tedious task over again. He had as much luck at winning Father's favour as we girls did of winning Mother's.

I never really saw much of my brother. And when I did, he was racing around the yard on yet another errand for Father. When Father left on some important farm mission or another, Keith took the chance to curl up on the living room couch and bask in the sun. He was exhausted from all his efforts to win over Father's approval. Keith ate like a pig. His growing body needed all the sustenance it could get. He was scrawny, spindly to the core but his work ethic grew strong under Father's severe guidance.

Keith and I had nothing in common, literally nothing. We'd stare each other down, calling each other swear words in the hollows of our minds. We were very territorial, claiming a special solidarity from each other.

But Joy's response shocked me. I thought there would be a bit more of a helper in her in my time of need, but she snubbed me and walked down the bus aisle to her crowd of friends. She was three years older than I. Our birthdays were two days apart in February. We shared a tiny room upstairs in the old farmhouse. A crack of space lay between our beds. An invisible line was drawn in the linoleum. I dared not step over it and she did not care to step into my disaster.

The lack of commonality due to age alone was apparent enough. While I loved my ability to create a cyclone in my part of the room, she was determined to impose army conditions on her side. She was short and slight while I grew taller every day. She doted on Mother's every word. I did my best to ignore her instructions. She moved into Mother's world. I snuck past her as fast as I could. Her ultimate obedience to the family structure kept her in a people-pleasing mode which I had actively rejected.

Above all else, she was a tattletale. She ratted me out to Mother with impeccable timing. It kept us at a comfortable distance and gave her power over me. She found great satisfaction in getting Keith to help me obey. His methods were far from tactful, to say the least.

There were moments of peace when I complied with her authority or she came over to the dark side in a moment of rebellion but they were rare. It was a rocky relationship but strangely enough, it was a relationship. Keith and I lived in the same house but Joy and I occasionally dwelt in some form of harmony. The moments of quiet understanding amidst a degree of separation grew in intensity as the years passed.

Today, I was just a lost little girl going to school for the first time. Sitting right at the front seat of the bus, I dared not look around. There was lots of chatter; everybody was getting to know each other anew. Inevitably, most of the chatter came from the girls, the boys sat slouched in the back seat, joggling up and down with each rut in the country road, the coolness oozing from their very pores.

There was only one other girl who was new to this whole routine. Cindy was her name and she was just as afraid as I was to turn around and see what was happening in the back. We both looked like two stiff china dolls staring straight ahead, looking neither to the left nor to the right. My feet wouldn't touch the ground so it was a good opportunity to swing them gently back and forth. It helped to calm my jittery nerves. I was glad to be all by myself on the big green plastic seat at the front of the bus. That meant that I could look out the big front window. We made a slow and deliberate turn in the road and there was the most breathtaking scene in the world. The September trees grew more and more colourful the closer we got...oranges... reds... deep yellows... all created a picture of dignity and calm on that narrow country road. I breathed them in and they filled me up. I had always seen those tall, glorious trees from ground level and now I saw them straight on, an amazing sight, so full of life.

SCHOOL TIME WONDERS

It was a two-room schoolhouse and Miss Moore taught Grade One to Grade Three. I was in Grade One and happy as a clam. Miss Moore became my absolute favourite teacher. She was the most awesome teacher in the whole wide world. She always looked you right in the eye when she was talking to you. If I had a question, she was sure to move quickly towards my desk. She nearly always put her hand on my shoulder as she explained the answers to my questions. I would nod politely whether I understood or not, smiling back all the while. She smiled too as she patted my back and returned to her big wooden desk at the front of the classroom.

The classroom was covered with all sorts of educational pictures. There was the alphabet with a picture for each letter. Then there was a big map of the world with a little red star for the province of Manitoba. The bulletin board at the front of the class had something new on it each day. Today we were learning about three-lettered words that ended with "at." The worksheets were passed down the rows of wooden desks until everyone received one. We had to find the corresponding picture to the word and spell it on the line beside on our matching work sheets. It was fun. Our hand printing had to be just perfect. There was an example of how to print each letter above the blackboard. I took advantage of having those letters up there printing slowly and carefully because I really wanted to impress Miss Moore.

SCHOOLYARD FUN

There was a large schoolyard with plenty of room to play in. There were swings and teeter-totters. The swings went high when you pumped like crazy. Sometimes we would stand behind the swing and toss it as hard as we could to see if we could get it up over the top bar of the swing set. It wasn't easy because the swing set was very high. Once we got it over a few times we would jump up on the swing and go for very short rides. We would have to swing back and forth with our legs at a mad pace to move just a short way. The bigger kids always had to get the swing back around and down for us because we were just too short.

The teeter-totter was another story. The only time I ever got on it was when a dear friend was on the other end. If a big bully got on with you, you were in huge trouble. Something called the bumps would give you splinters in your hands and butt as you hung on for dear life. There was always that extra bounce at the end that jarred your head and crossed your eyes. There was a much better survival rate if a friend beat the bully to the seat.

If your friends were all playing somewhere else on the schoolyard, it was just as good to take a running start at the teeter-totter, landing somewhere in the middle, all the while trying to balance in the centre. Once exact balance was achieved, the teeter-totter would rock back and forth gently while you tried not to go overboard one way or the other. It wasn't easy creating that comfortable slow sway. It took some moments of awkward balancing before it would equalize out into tranquil, slow movement. Of course, often a great big fifth grader would come along pushing you off and claim the long narrow board as his own. Although I was always tempted to try to get the board back, I never did. Instead, I would walk slowly to the back of the schoolyard, nursing my deep wounds over having been a pushover once again.

There was usually a hearty game of Kick-the-Can happening in the field beyond the small schoolhouse. This was one of the best games in the world. Everybody would gather around in a huddle to start. I can't exactly remember how we decided who would search the yard first; all I know is that it very rarely ended up being me.

This was one place where the older kids felt sorry for me, even after I was in grade three or four. Once we made a decision about who was it, they would start counting as fast as they could up to one hundred. Everyone else would disperse as rapidly as they could into the nearby bushes, hoping not to be caught first. The rusty old peanut butter can was left nearby the kid who was counting. Slowly but surely the unlucky counter would try to find all of us.

I was fortunate most of the time to end up being one of the last participants to be found. I knew the importance of remaining in one place and staying ever so quiet. I rarely had the courage to run up to the rusty tin can and give it that mighty kick. My way of participating in the game was to disappear into the flora and fauna around me. While the frantic counter was off finding the others, I would lie low in the scrub, the pokey underbrush stabbing at me until I learnt to grow still. The uncomfortable jabs grew faint against my young skin and I would lie and look up as far as I could into the heavens, counting clouds, realizing anew the blueness of the sky. With no intention of leaving my glorious found spot, I would begin envisioning clouds of animals. Giraffes with their necks stretched out long and dark grey elephants sauntering along, orangutans beating their proud chests and massive hippos waddling in the sloppy mud holes.

I would wait silently while some brave soul would venture out from his hiding place and race my classmate to the can. The idea of the whole game was for someone to kick the can before the fellow who was "it", so those who had been caught could excape and he would have to be "it" all over again. It was one of my favourite games because it inspired me to practice my hiding techniques.

I was extremely skilled in the art of invisibility. I could make myself disappear on command. This talent grew stronger and stronger as the days of my life grew. It was almost a hallowed feeling. I became one with nature and close to the heavens and even closer to a God I hoped existed. The feelings of contentment brought me to a higher place, settling in my tired soul. I had created a precision art with the passage of time and I needed this crutch like never before at this moment. However, as my school years progressed, the enjoyment of the nature around me during these games of Kick-the-Can came to an abrupt end.

THE HALL

Although my first days of school in Grade One with Miss Moore were such a success, by the time I got to fourth grade, things went strangely awry. My new teacher, Mrs. Firth, was impeccable and orderly in every way. Unlike my dear Miss Moore, she was a strict disciplinarian. We sat in desks that were in straight rows. Sliding the desk from one side to the other in order to see the blackboard better was not allowed. Turning around to ask a classmate a question was a big no-no. Any kind of fidgeting drove Mrs. Firth out of her mind. We were all to sit up straight and tall in our desks and the only thing to be moving was our yellow HB2 pencils. Her writing on the board was as straight as an arrow (no guidelines required, of course). Most of my other teachers' writing slid slowly down to one side of the board, but not hers.

I did almost anything I could to cause a commotion, simply to let her know she wasn't in complete control, usually fraternizing with those around me. There were three grades in this classroom. My grade sat in the first two rows. There were six of us, two boys and four girls. We were the biggest grade in the school. Sometimes children were kept back a grade or skipped depending on how many kids there were in the grade. The girl who lived across the road from us was kept back a year and moved into my grade while Jo was moved up a year. She actually skipped a grade because she would have been the only one in her grade. The two boys were super short and we girls secretly giggled at their plight in life.

The hallway had varying colours of beige linoleum in it. I was no stranger to these squares of chipped linoleum. Sitting calmly in my desk doing my work, my classmate behind me was continually trying to get me to speak. Speaking meant you landed in the hallway immediately. I was on my best behaviour today, and besides, it was quite a challenge not to give in to my classmate's attempts to get me into trouble. But eventually she got the best of me by taking a pencil, a sharp one, I might add, and stabbing it right into my bare knee (I still have a bluish scar from it). I was wearing my plaid skirt that day. She pulled the pencil out in a shot and put it in her wooden desk. I howled in pain, which of course got the whole room's attention. The teacher needed to only look at me with her eyes. I was bound to the hallway for the second time that day.

I obediently pulled my desk through the maze of the other desks as the others remained stationary, with quizzical looks in their eyes. Through the door, those brazen square tiles where staring me in the face. In a way I was glad to have escaped that dull classroom with the constraining teacher at the front. Instead I could dwell on the nifty little spots in the school. It was a two-room schoolhouse with a small library. It sat in the middle of a small town surrounded by rows of bushes. They defined the schoolyard with its lax boundaries. Escape was simple, at least in my mind. I could see all these things inside and outside the window. They were comforting; no one could tell me what to do in the hallway.

These extended periods of freedom when Mrs. Firth sent me out into the hall lasted half an hour, and I relished in them. It was great to be able to look out of the row of windows along one side of the hallway. The scenery held a beauty all its own, whether it was winter or summer. I loved the freedom of being able to stare dreamily out the window, thinking of whatever I wanted.

Every once in a while, I would sneak away from my wooden desk and get a drink of water from the fountain at the side of the hall. This was tricky, though. If I were caught away from my desk, I would get the strap. Mrs. Firth was heavy-handed for a woman, probably even more so because she was the principal. After all, she had a reputation to keep up.

Mrs. Firth eventually found me to be so frustrating that she put me in the front of the classroom. My constant whispering and plotting of practical jokes became too much for her. That meant that pretty well every afternoon I was eventually relegated to the hallway, along with my desk, for punishment. Of course, for me, this was no punishment at all. I rarely did the work she assigned to me. I dreamt of everything and anything. I became completely unaware of my surroundings. I created innovative designs in my head, and then drew them out on paper as best I could. I even thought of ways to get back at Mrs. Firth. Perhaps a Whoopee cushion on her chair would scare her, or I could encourage the flies to come in at recess. They would buzz around her head, driving her into a state of madness. Although she would be well equipped with a fly swatter, the flies would elude her sad attempts to kill them.

Once I was even brave enough to pop a piece of bubble gum directly at the back of her head. I doodled in my notebook, driving her crazy because, in her standard of perfection, every student should have a nice neat page with white margins on either side. Special messages were often waiting for her on the blackboard, the whole class giggling at them as she strutted into the classroom. A classmate of mine played dirty tricks on her for me, too.

I went through this routine for three years. I am not sure how I passed my grades, with all the free time in the hall, but pass I did.

During those years, the only part I liked about school was singing along with the radio. Every Friday afternoon we would all gather round as the broadcast began. We started out with do-re-me and slowly progressed to a real song with a real tune. My ability to sing in tune was pathetic at best. I could not sing a note if my life depended on it. But the other children made up for the poor quality of my voice.

PENNER'S PENALTIES

There was a narrow piano room with a small window at the very end of the hall in our elementary school. Mother made me take piano lessons. If I thought Mrs. Firth was strict, I soon discovered that she was nothing like Mrs. Penner, the music teacher. I was in for a rude awakening as those sweet notes hit the keyboard. I hated the army drill voice that went along with every lesson. I never learnt the dynamics of the instrument. Rather, if I made a mistake, she would go over my mistake on the piano, teaching me the right way. I would follow her lead and get it right through pure imitation. I played my way through to Grade Five in the Leila Fletcher School of Music and I grew more and more bored with the lessons each day. I was so glad when the day came that Mother finally acquiesced and said I could quit.

COMMANDING OFFICER

It was a Saturday, the one and only day my big brother could sleep in, all of us could, for that matter. Father woke up at 5 a.m., his usual. He had gone out and puttered around the yard. He came back at 7 a.m. yelling up the stairs. It wasn't very pleasant or necessary from my point of view. Nevertheless, Keith jumped into action, trembling at his voice. He knew there would be trouble today. Not two minutes later, there was another loud call. Father was in fine form already having been up for two hours; doing his best to antagonize us all out of our cozy beds. When Keith got down to the main floor, he realized it was raining and he wondered why Father was in such a hurry. There would be no harvesting today. He was chided for not being up earlier as he clomped down the stairs, he was ordered to go outside and clean the bin on the left side in the big red granary.

Now this granary was very old and full of rats and mice. It had narrow little openings to crawl through in order to get into the bin itself. The opening was about two feet wide and not quite three feet high. You had to jump up into it, hang by your stomach, perched on the window-type ledge, unable to do anything but balance awkwardly trying to get your bearings. Eventually you could do nothing but fall headfirst into the bin. It was dark and the smell was intolerable as there was rotting grain in every corner. The whole building wasn't exactly waterproof. Keith went as fast as he could before his Father could berate him and give him a shove. This meant no breakfast and a lot of hard work before noon.

Father had decided to prepare the bins for harvest. Luckily, Keith knew where the shovels and such were in order to do the job to Father's satisfaction. There were no dust masks and no proper clothing to relieve him from the constant itching of the barley. It would be a long, arduous day. However, it was better to be in that dirty old bin than anywhere near Father. Keith knew nothing else in his mind than that he was a stupid idiot who could do nothing right. In fact, he knew he would never clean the bin to Father's demands and that he would have to do it several times over before he got it up to this highest standard. He had been unlucky today.

Nevertheless, it seemed we had all been unlucky. Mother was next at around 8 a.m. Father came in the door once again. He found his wife sitting and drinking coffee at the kitchen table. He wasn't going to stand for that. In his mind, he called her lazy repeatedly. She smiled at him offering him his own cup of caffeine. He was unimpressed and told her he needed a part from the John Deere store for the old combine and if she didn't get it in a hurry he would lose all opportunity to fix it before the rain stopped. Mother patiently took down the part number and tried not to listen as he ranted and raved. Her coffee had been ruined and her state of peace was now gone. She got up in silence and walked out the door. That left my sister, my little brother and me to terrorize out of sleep. We had heard all the commotion and covered our heads with our pillows. No sense in listening to it all before our names were called. In the end, Joy was to go out and help Keith with the bin. She hated the bins and I cannot say I blamed her. She came out dirty and smelly, tired and grumpy. Since Mother wasn't back from the John Deere parts store yet, Joy had to make lunch for the obedient crew. I was lucky that way because I had allergies so I usually had to stay inside the house and clean up the dirt that Father left behind. I was astounded at how peaceful the house was once Father left.

I was free to do as I pleased until the sound of his voice was heard again. I was to go with him to the shed and hand him tools at the appropriate time. I knew little about what a wrench or a bolt was. I inevitably got it wrong and was pounded on in one way or the other. There really was no safe place. That is, until my younger brother Andy came bounding in the shed door to rescue me. He had a much better grasp of these things. He pointed to the appropriate item with confidence and I gingerly handed it to Father, hoping he was right. This was a much better system. I was somewhat hopeful that I would make it through the day unscathed by Father's anger.

EARLY TO RISE

The passage of time grew redundant in its predictability. Every spring Mother got baby chicks and we always ended up with a rooster. The call of the roosters could be heard half way across the yard. They perched on the roof of the old porch. To me it was as if those roosters were in the next room cock-a-doodle-dooing out the glory of a new day. They were downright annoying with their insistent racket. Why would I wake up when it was a perfectly good day to be in bed? My preference was to remain sound asleep, comfy under my covers, my head included.

Father always got up at the crack of dawn, jumping into his greasy, green overalls and heading out the door onto the porch. He was ever eager to start his day. He was an extremely determined man. He would stomp confidently to the shed, finding something that needed to be greased or oiled. All the while Mother was kept hidden away in the house trying to make good on her husband's strong work ethic. In the farmhouse entrance, he would greet the morning with a deep, contented breath and attach his old worn work boots to his feet.

Listening for Mother's voice to come hollering loud and clear up the stairs, declaring the new day just as surely as the old roosters, was not much different than listening for Father's. Every day she would lean over the bottom of the dark, narrow staircase leading to the upstairs of our house. She had her hand on her hip (at least that's the way I imagined her). Twisting her neck around the corner and up the stairs in the general direction of the three bedrooms we inhabited, she gave the command, "Time to rise and shine." Sometimes she sounded happy about the new day and sometimes just plain frustrated. You could pretty well tell what your day would be like by the tone of her voice.

Now when it came to my preference, I preferred to hear a light-hearted sense of joy in Mother's tone of voice. I tossed a dice in my mind to see which one it would be, for the better or for the worse. No matter what I decided to myself, I went down the hall stairs with fear and trepidation. I couldn't help believing that frustration was inevitable; that Mother would find something to pick on or complain about so I got a little nervous going down those cracked linoleum stairs.

Most days, I was the first one down the stairs and dressed, not because I was eager to listen to the rich deep resonance of Father's voice, but because I was eager to get the whole thing over with. I might add that I pretty well wore the same thing every day, so it was a no-brainer about what to wear.

Each morning, I would grab the well-worn banister as I went down the stairs. I worked hard at trying to shake it free from its moorings as I moved it back and forth violently. You see, it had always been wobbly so this had been my challenge for a long while. When I was done with that, my childish hand slid down it. The splinters in my palm drew blood but I didn't even notice after a while. Most of the varnish was gone off the wooden banister, creating a treacherous road map down the stairs. Reaching the bottom of the stairs, I would peek around the corner deftly and find out where Mother was working in her tiny kitchen.

Her tousled hair, slippers and green velour housecoat were telltale signs that she hadn't been up long herself. She moved swiftly around the kitchen, setting the table, putting on coffee, setting out cereal. She was a regular hub of activity. I would search intently into her face for some sign of displeasure. On days when I saw her smiling softly to herself, I would confidentally move forward from my hiding place and finding my chair, sit down at the kitchen table.

While I sat there, I would watch Mother scurry around, and in my mind try to figure out what the hurry was. She exhausted me by her constant movement. There was no hesitation as she went from station to station, completing her morning routine. She was on automatic pilot. Either it was very important to get us out of the house and to school or there was something much deeper at stake. I could never figure it out so instead I would wait impatiently, hands folded on the table, rolling thumb over thumb. Even though my hands where folded, my legs swung back and forth at a violent rate. I would sit there trying to prepare myself for the morning family devotional.

Usually, Joy and Keith came jumping down the stairs two at a time into the tiny kitchen, Andy was always the slow poke bringing up the rear. The boys never combed their hair and often wore the same thing they had on from the day before. In fact, Andy would wear the same sweater all week long if Mother would let him. Joy, on the other hand, was meticulously dressed; nothing was out of place. Me, well, I was somewhere in between. Let me get something straight, I was not in my brother's category of cleanliness. I didn't stink because I forgot to use my deodourant or anything. Taking their seats, everyone, including Mother, would sit "perfectly still" waiting for Father to take his seat of honour - a ripped, brown chair, dirty from his constant work in the fields.

Some days, Mother had to call Father for breakfast more than once in order to get him to come to the house from the shed. This was accomplished by the ringing of a big bell on the porch. It was right next to the entrance door and there was many a time we children would beg for a turn to ring it; big, brass and loud. Father would come sauntering out from the shed where he was working on his morning assignment, and cross the yard in his own good time. His boots remained on the porch outside the door. His grimy hands where washed with a smelly lotion from a red bottle. It got rid of all the grease and dirt imbedded in the strongly creased hands.

Sitting down he would take up his glasses. He tried to find a clean place on his greasy uniform and proceeded to wipe his glasses "clean". Then he would begin to read aloud in an authoritative voice.

There was always a verse or two from the Bible that I really couldn't make any sense of. The verses were always in italics. I wasn't sure what that meant either. In spite of all our hard realities, Father still announced, with Bible in hand, "Love your neighbour as yourself" or "Love the Lord your God with all your heart, soul and mind."

After the verses came a reading from **Our Daily Bread**, a booklet which was supposed to help us understand the Bible but often to my child's mind, made it more obscure than ever.

My attention grew exponentially less, the longer the reading lasted. These spiritual lessons I took in fell on deaf ears. Instead, I stared out the window at the trees, at the birds, anything that crossed my path. I would catch words. Love... Faith... Patience... Joy... The words were beyond my grasp, leaving me lost, bewildered. It seemed that these profundities were the contradiction of my small life.

There weren't any pictures or anything like that so mostly my confusion over the passage grew. I really don't think these readings were meant for children. The words were humongous and as far as I could tell, out of order. I had more important things to think about other than Calvinistic interpretations of Christianity, such as who it would be that I would sit beside during gym and who would I play with at recess. These were the things my eager mind wanted to know.

Andy responded much the same way to these devotional times. He did more playing; swinging his legs, inspecting his cutlery, pointing at the orioles outside, than he did listening to the forever devotional, smiling sweetly the whole while.

Days passed by, the same routine over and over. Up for breakfast, get dressed quickly. Orange and red matched, didn't they? Downstairs, usually sliding on the banister, to sit on an old kitchen chair, aluminum legs curled around an antique gold, vinyl seat and back. We prepared for the family devotional using the Bible and the small pamphlet, sitting perfectly, still waiting for Father to take his cherished seat of honour. Each day He took up his glasses and read in an authoritative voice. Verses from the Bible were prepared ahead of time by finding the appropriate passage. The King James Version brought much confusion with all its "thees" and "thous." Then came the profound explanation of the passage from **Our Daily Bread**, the tiny booklet that came in the mail each month, for free, of course. It sat in a place of honour on the kitchen counter for the rest of the day.

This was our "boring as ever" routine. Every single morning we prepared for the brilliance of a new day. Even now, I can remember the wondrous sights and smells of the round breakfast table. I can't help but be amazed at how vividly every detail comes to mind, as if it were permanently seared on my memory, a moment of clarity in a childhood that has largely slipped away. In my memory, this daily ritual of Bible meditations is part of what made home life even more of a paradox.

Just the thought of being near Father created an extreme angst in me. I climbed inside myself, finding a comfort I rarely found in the outside world. I couldn't understand whether religion or action came first. I heard vile things about the neighbours. I felt the judgments placed upon my soul in everyday life. I felt the crack of the leather belt on my back, knowing it would leave deep purple wounds. And suddenly religion didn't make much sense. Was it found on a piece of thin paper surrounded by gold and bound in a red leather book forgotten on the cupboard for the day? Was it loudly uttered only when an angry, demanding person needed to obtain selfish, unhindered power, for the sake of justifying his evil deeds? Did saying something profoundly meaningful to the one who suffered at its use somehow absolve the abuser? None of this created any longing in me to know more about religion; maybe more about Jesus, but certainly not religion.

To this day, I do not remember even one of those long exegetical ramblings from that wordy booklet. It wasn't bread for me. I preferred my peanut butter and grape jelly. And that's exactly what I got after the reading and the prayer. The prayer was more or less the same every day. I had it memorized and repeated it dutifully with one hand ready on the butter knife eager to obtain the first piece of homemade bread, lightly toasted.

BUSH ATTACK

I saw the form of his body coming, stealthily towards me. I breathed a deep sigh and groaned inwardly. My plans had been foiled. In my own little world I would have become as an ant on a hill, but there was no doubt he had his eye on me as he ambled through the brush.

He was dressed sloppily. I could smell the body odour mixed with the chores he did daily. The cows and the chickens had soaked so far into his jacket no amount of washing could erase the permanent barnyard smell. His jeans where filthy, especially around the knees, his hair unkempt, and his face, well, it was determined. A crude smile spread in delight across his face. It was telltale of the events that were about to come.

During the usual recess game of Kick-the-Can, I had run too far away from the rest of the group, leaving myself vulnerable. The closer he got, the clearer his face became. His coal-dark eyes were filled with the thrill of the hunt. There was nothing amorous about his stance. In fact, his red checkered jacket was already thrown to the ground. The prickles would stab at his soft, teenage skin if he tore off his shirt, so he pulled it up as far as he dared.

Once again, he had found his prey lying still in the grass. There was nowhere for me to go. I was stuck on the forest floor, glued to the rotting leaves and dirt around me. My safe haven was gone. He advanced. We both knew the routine. He rarely took his time, instead forcing his way on me with a clear, single-minded goal. If I resisted, life would become even harsher for me. His mockery and scorn would follow me around the schoolyard.

And so I lay there, in what was once a safe haven, and allowed the hallowed ground to become filthy, filthy beyond what this world could bring. He pushed my shirt up rubbing his scrawny chest on my favourite shirt. He mumbled and whined to himself, finding some unknown pleasure in my forced demise. Then he stood up quickly, doing some sort of bohemian dance; he pulled down his pants to his knees and ripped my pants down as far as they would go with all the prickles and brush. The look on his face was horrifying. All his basest instincts had brought a sick feeling to my delicate stomach. Pushing my shirt up and slobbering, ripping his tongue across my small chest. The rubbing was ceaseless until at last he succeeded in his conquest. He lay in the brambles for a minute or two, knowing he had conquered his helpless prey. Then he was up and away, gathering his things as he went.

No one would ever believe me if I told his dirty little secrets. I created my own world while the sickening deed was performed. I rose up into the air and watched from above the earth. I pretended to see only the nature surrounding me. Now instead of watching the clouds, I was moving along with them. Soaring high through the air brought the safety and comfort I longed for while the grunting and groaning of my classmate heightened. As he flopped down beside me I gradually became one with the earth again. I pretended he was my nearest and dearest friend and that we had just shared secrets and laughs together as he lay there writhing in some sort of animalistic delight. My innocence proved of value to me, for I didn't have the faintest clue what had just happened. I had spent far too much time trying to push it all as far away as possible.

Disappearing into myself, then up and away into the clear blue sky once again, was the only way I had of warding off the evil of everyday living. I would come out from my shell only if I perceived the slightest hint of safety, and that was only on a rare occasion. I felt deep distress over accepting the fact that to be crushed and pushed down was my lot in life. It created an emptiness that relegated me to strategies for living that came only from my imagination. Becoming invisible, sometimes even to my own existence, was my favoured way of bringing a wavering balance to my starving soul. Otherwise, the helplessness and confusion of living life without solid security could only bring me to my knees. Anxiety was a complexity, was I the guilty one or was my transgressor? I did not know. With the help of my elevated imagination I kept hope alive. Running away gave me only temporary relief, but retreating into myself was a far better strategy; no one knew I had gone away, and they made no attempts to bring me back.

The problem with becoming invisible is that eventually you are left with a lack of connection to the world around you, left in a place no one knows you.

JUNIOR HIGH CHAOS

"Joy lies in the fight, in the attempt, in the suffering involved, not in the victory itself."

Mahatma Gandhi

Graduating into Junior High was quite the shock to my system. My best friend took up smoking. There was a smoking pad at the entrance of the school and all the friendly fumes would waft through the entrance way to the school. Smoking was never anything I desired to learn how to do. Watching my teenage classmates standing in the bitter breeze of winter sucking on a stick and blowing out a puff only lessened my desire. I was always the oldest in my class so my best friend would get me to hold her cigarette whenever the teachers came around. Other girls who were younger quickly caught on and used my welcoming fingers to house yet more nicotine. I gave up going out to spend time with her after a while and decided on the library as my next noon hour hangout. This was much more to my liking. I could sit at a table and read to my heart's content. Did it really have to matter that I was alone again?

Junior High was made up of one big open area. There were six classrooms with grey fabric partitions in between each one. Noise traveled well and it was easy to listen in on the teaching session next to you. If you were lucky enough to get a back seat before everyone else stole the good spots, you could even spend time watching what was going on in the class next door. Chaos reigned whenever a teacher left the room to get forgotten school materials. Erasers, pencils, you name it flew through the air. No one stayed in his or her desk. If the teacher next door was gone too, you could invite yourself into the unruly class and take in the frivolous activities of the young at heart. The open area was not very conducive to discipline or intent study.

I had learnt my lessons well in elementary school. Whispering to the person next to you, throughout the lecture, was one way to make the day go by faster if learning was not your objective. My intention was harmless but the sound of my voice must have sounded defiant. A good friend of mine sat just behind me in Social Studies class. I often turned around and chatted with her, much to the teacher's dismay. On more than one occasion he grew hostile and, taking a wooden yardstick up in his hand, he whacked me across the shoulders with it. Needless to say, I was quiet for the rest of the class. A certain understanding had been reached for the moment, but I broke that understanding many a time. The lesson was always the same. The wooden yardstick, with its inch long measurements, was well used, but not for its true use.

I have to admit there was something about German class and German teachers that was insane from day one. First, we had Mr. Rempel. He was a crumpled up little old man who should have been at home, sound asleep in front of his television. His grey hair was wavy and sat just below his eye line. He had these huge glasses that took up his entire face. He never cracked a smile. In fact, I'm pretty sure he could hardly speak English. His shirt was usually buttoned up wrong and he looked like he could keel over at any minute.

The schedule of the class went this way. He sat at his desk until we were all quiet, which was approximately ten minutes. Then he would look down at his textbook and say, "Turn to page fifty-two of your textbook and practice the German words found there." That was it. Then he went back into la-la-land and within a few minutes no one was studying the assigned page. Sometimes we got so loud; teachers from other classes came walking by and told us to shut up. All the while Mr. Rempel slept on. He even snored and mumbled in his sleep. I believed this to be an excellent way to learn German. He certainly held the highest standards for his students.

The next German teacher was equally as interesting. She was very young and very plump. Her name was Miss Schreiber. She had short, dark hair, all curled under at the ends. She was a cheery type for the most part. She wrote notes on the board and there was a certain amount of teaching going on. But it was extremely easy to taunt her right out of the classroom. We bothered her with inane questions and made stupid comments. We pushed her to her limits until she couldn't handle us any more. Then she would run crying from the classroom, unable to control herself. She never returned again that same day, so we had a heyday at her expense and gained an extra free period.

The next teacher was a true German. By that, I mean he hailed from the country of Germany. He had a strong accent, sometimes hard to understand. Unlike the first two teachers, he was extremely attentive. If we had trouble with the linguistics of the language he was right there helping us out.

It wasn't long before I began to notice that he helped the girls out more than the guys. He had a particular propensity to come to my desk to make sure I was excelling in the art of the German language. It all started out very innocently or so I thought. He slowly graduated to putting his arm around my shoulder while he was answering my slightest beck and call.

The slight nudging of the breasts came next as he released his hold on my shoulder. Somewhere down the slippery slope, the graduals disappeared and he was openly fondling me in class. Everybody knew it but pretended not to. Everybody knew but nobody really cared. This was the plight of being one of this man's favoured students. I cannot say that this had a particularly good outcome in my life. My strong propensity to become invisible embedded itself even further into the fabric of my being.

MUDDY RIVERS

staring at the blackboard, eyes blank, performance impeccable, erect in my chair

feet planted firmly on the floor, singled out, for his good pleasure

studious, alert, with hollow mind

praying for redemption, pleading for a canopy to wrap its arms around me

for a barrier, impenetrable, unapproachable, desire reigns

an awkward defense lifts its head, self-protection of soul hardens my thoughts,

an invisible line creates insulation, safety factors in, a feeling of wholeness

pushes away unpleasant rumblings in my soul

a repulsion so strong twists my insides, sickening my soul, shaking me

I am confined, confined to my own device and to my chair

rejecting· the taste, the taste of sensuality, stomping out the tingling slurs in my mind

they are a tribute to the senses turned off like a tap, sexuality sickens

poured in a funnel, dripping with hate and repulsion

oozing out certain death the tap rusts shut bringing relief

yet an unseen river grows ominously, putrid, muddy

promiscuity settles on the water, charred with impurity, the stench unbearable

blind eyes stare, filthy hands stir up dark recesses of the soul

searching, groping, confusion replaces calmness

torrential onslaughts pour down, floundering, creating pools

dark and heavy, formidable and cold

terror ceases the day pushing away tranquility, sense of self is replete, grasping for logic

some reason, mad attempts intensify, rays of hope gone, the lost lays unfound

impatient searching, fumbling, shaking hands

silence reigns, heavier, heavier, weighted down, by an unseen force

falling backwards, sucked down and in

terror destroys, arms flail, feet bound, motionless, eyes clenched

wild thoughts singing out, "Remove me. Remove me. Remove me."

silence remains, self-will resumes

willpower removes all doubt drowning out deception

caught yet resigned to freedom, lied to, taunted but strong of heart

pushing against the force, treading water, struggling towards safety

lying exhausted, alone, beached, relieved

eyes closing, peace descends down.

relaxation and rest, relaxation and rest, unguarded thoughts

a wind whispers standing over me, his voice jittery, sickeningly so

a pleasant touch, a twisted smile, an invitation

nausea ripples through me, I smile politely, stymied.

unsure, stripped of reprieve, the river beckons, his hand slides down my back

the dark water invites me, his eyes undress me,

I slide into the murky water, it is safer there,

calm and reassuring

RAIN, RAIN, RAIN

The weather radio that Father had bought predicted rain, well, not just rain, but weather patterns that were particularly helpful in maintaining his summer crops. The voice was kind of funny. It sounded like a robot, with the man's tone never changing. He actually sounded bored as he relayed the information. He was also very nasally with a deep, deep voice.

I smiled to myself every time the little radio turned on. Today the winds were gusting hard, causing driving rain. That didn't mean very good things for the tender shoots of grain that were sprouting up in the freshly seeded fields. Father looked worried as he listened to the forecast. He had worked hard planting the tiny seeds in the ground and he wouldn't be too impressed with the rain and wind crushing his blessed handiwork.

The truth is I wasn't thinking too hard about all that. Instead, there was a sense of anticipation in me. I loved the sound of the rain on the farmhouse roof. Starting out slowly, tapping gently on the windowpanes then growing stronger and louder. The temptation to move outside and enjoy the gloomy clouds became irresistible. I would stare out the window enraptured by the sight and sound.

Soon my parents, Andy and I went out onto the patio and sat on the old church bench that I had painted a rusty brown colour. We watched the rain pour down. The sound of it pounding against the plastic yellow roof above was ear-shattering. Just as we were enjoying the steady stream falling down, a huge clap of thunder sounded with a fury, very close to us. I jumped up and shrieked all at once. Then I moved over to the edge of the patio. I looked for the corresponding lightning but I had just missed it. Now I decided to look intently into the sky until I could see lightening crashing through the clouds.

Suddenly I saw the flash. I was as amazed as ever to see the beautiful line of electricity light up the sky. It was what I had been waiting for. I was satisfied now, suddenly feeling the cold night temperature seep through my skin. I sat back down, trying to be brave in the dark and the cold but I had gotten what I came for. I was ready for the warmth of the house. Maybe if I asked nicely Mother would make some hot chocolate for Andy and me. We could drink it from the safety and shelter of the house, where we could still watch the rain from the kitchen window and see the windmill turning round and round at a furious pace. This time the storm would stay outside where it belonged. I would remain warm and content inside.

FATHER AND ME

"It is poverty to decide that a child must die so that you may live as you wish."

Mother Teresa

Some things in this life hold a sense of time. There is regularity and an order to them. Our lives were broken up into seeding time, growing time and harvest time. Other than that, it did not seem like much else mattered, at least to Father anyway. Of course, there was a host of things that had to be done before seeding and one of those things was to fine-tune all the machinery. I continually mixed up the names of everything, calling a harrow a seeder and a seeder a harrow. Truth be told, about the only thing that interested me was climbing along the top of these machines while Father got out the grease gun and maneuvered down on his hands and knees, painstakingly greasing every joint.

There was still snow on the ground in little bits and it was below zero but that never deterred Father from getting an early start. The cold that seeped into his bones from the frozen ground went unnoticed as he worked feverishly. The arthritis that had grown in his bones from his insistence not to wear any protective gear was ignored. His mad pace was not only acceptable but also desired.

He never admitted to this aloud, but he considered being the first one on the land in the spring and the first one finished harvesting in the fall to be his greatest achievement.

There were no words exchanged between us. There was no friendly camaraderie, just silence. We were each in our own little worlds, oblivious to the rest of the world. I went about the solemn business of climbing onto the seeder. I always started with it first because the hardest thing about it was the climbing up. Falling off the long, narrow machine was just a bit of a joke.

On one of those days, I put one foot up as high as I could onto a narrow ledge I had found in some nook or cranny on the monstrosity of a machine and felt for a handhold. I hoisted my body up to the next level and stood firmly on the foothold I had found. A sigh of relief escaped my lips. I had conquered the first leg of the journey, now for the rest. It did not take long before I reached the summit. Standing proudly at the top, I crossed my arms and looked across the mighty farmland. Larger than life, the landscape spread before me. The dog was resting lazily in the sun beside the shed. The clangs and gongs of Father hard at work just below rang out. The cats were wandering the land, scoping out each section for fresh meat. The birds flew high in the air, then dove down low, playing the game of a stunt plane.

There were so many things to see and hear atop my new found perch, I was unaware of the imminent danger that would befall me if I continued to look up at the sky instead of down at my feet. There was many a time I banged a knee or scraped an arm by falling off the seeder, but falling off of the harrows created the potential for an even greater set of injuries.

The harrow had many prongs with sharp blades at the bottom of each one. There was no flat surface on the top to walk along, like there was on the seeder. On the harrows, you sprang gingerly from surface to surface. There were huge gaps in between, making it next to impossible to navigate across without harming yourself in one way or another.

That did not deter me. I moved in a crooked path, jumping and wobbling along, balancing on one leg, then the other, almost falling, gaining new balance, finding another direction in my search for the next perfect spot. This continued until I had either fallen through a crack or landed safely on the other side. Even though my life flashed before my eyes many times, I still stumbled courageously across the structure, planning each step with the care of a child.

To this day I cannot figure out why Father allowed this behaviour for there were many times I went running to the house, scraped and bleeding, with big gashes on my arms and legs. I don't believe he even noticed when I fell off his beloved equipment; he was too caught up in the pressures and excitement of spring.

This odd behaviour between Father and me existed because of his inability to have a relationship with anybody but himself and his farm. Being close to him physically was the only way I could think of to establish any sort of bond with him. It was as close as I could come to the existence of love. I had to pretend that I was important to him in some way. With the nearness of his presence, I could contrive a twisted sense of belonging. However cold and distant it was, it provided me with some sense of comfort.

Father never knew anything much about me personally, but that didn't really seem to matter to him. My purpose was to provide him with the goods and services he needed to keep his farm afloat. Warmth and care came a distant second.

EXPECTATIONS

One day everything was right, and we all basked in Father's approval. The next day was different; the bins were not cleaned to Father's expectation. He had found scraps of molding grain in one of the corners of the century old bin. His voice filled our yard with terror.

I peeked out from the safety of the house window. Keith was standing in the middle of the yard with Father frantically looking around himself for some instrument to use on Keith to teach him a good lesson. The piece of wood he finally found carried a deadly, rusty old nail in it. It was not that Keith was not used to Father's unwarranted behaviour by now, but he found himself cowering in fear. Not shortly after, he started running as fast as he could with Father right after him. My eyes were glued to the scene. Certainly, nothing good could come from any of this.

Father took aim and walloped Keith broadside on the back, but one whack was not enough for Father. Because he was faster and stronger than Keith, he eventually caught up to his son, grabbed him by the arm and dragged him towards himself. I couldn't see the look on my brother's face but I could well imagine the terror in his soul. Father never even flinched as he brought the wooden piece down on his back again and again. I waited for a scream from Keith, for a sign that he was still breathing, alive; but there was nothing. The silence of this abuse was unbearable.

SHUFFLING

sweetness of sound and the sun, the rocks and the frogs, only the sound of the wind blowing across the fields

and the devastation of my own thoughts, that Amazing Grace with its sweetness of sound had disappeared

sloughing along on the Big, Gravel Road, shuffling along in my too big shoes wandering

looking for frogs and pebbles, finding that perfect pebble

smooth and round, my greatest challenge, I did my best to concentrate on my surroundings

whisking away the memories of the day, but the ache I felt all over would not go away

constant anxiety never told, helplessness to control the endless mayhem

trapped in a body unable to free itself from certain destruction, free self from thoughts of abuse staring me in the face

the smell of cookies at my aunt's did not entice me, I wanted nothing more than to be free from the torments of my mind

but there is no one, no one to free me, no one to sing a lullaby to bring peace and rest

copyright©1997 Gayleen Gaeke

COLD AND DAMP

"I have found it easier to identify with the characters who verge upon hysteria, who were frightened of life, who were desperate to reach out to another person. But seemingly fragile people are the strong people really."

Tennessee Williams

I was pulled down the rickety stairs, usually by the scruff of my neck. His lanky body pulled me along behind him. His one step meant two for me. The dog fought for me in his own manner, sinking his teeth into my opponent's boney leg. My tormentor did not hide his hatred for me nor the dog. A good, swift kick took care of the mangy mutt for awhile. He went whirling down the rugged, once red, stairs; yelping on his way.

All this time a figure skulked at the top of the stairs. We played a game of peek-a-boo. But the shape of the face was too recognizable. It was obvious who began the whole thing. I had my ways of getting back, and knew I would use them to my advantage. The stick-in-the-mud had proved once again there was no power to be had alone, and yet this helplessness was my demise.

This looming figure was cruel in word, calling me things I had never heard. Sometimes I fought back and sometimes I went reluctantly but never did I lose control. My spirit was wild and strong.

But the fear of it still creeps in sometimes.

It was like being in a dungeon. Cold and damp, I lay on the floor incapable of moving, paralyzed in my mind. My hands were tied behind my back so tightly they bit into my skin. The harsh ropes were bound at my ankles. They made a deep red impression on my tender skin. The darkness overwhelmed me. I was mute and blind. All I had were my thoughts of panic. I was cut off from any sense of reality. Nothing seemed to exist but this torment. I struggled to be free from my bonds but I couldn't budge the ropes.

Eventually I gave up and lay helplessly on the dirty, cement floor. The room had many names: the potato room, the freezer room and the canning room. I could hear the hum of the freezer as it came on. I tried to concentrate on it and pretend I was somewhere else. Somewhere the cold couldn't touch me but it kept seeping back in. A dirty old rag was wound tightly around my eyes. I struggled to break free of my bonds once more but it only proved fruitless. I knew I would be left alone to rot in this dank, dark room. I knew that the passage of time was taking place but all sense of it was gone to me. The smell of the earth lay heavy in the air. I knew instinctively where everything was. I tried to picture the narrow room in my mind. I did not want to feel like I was in a vacuum of space where no one could reach me. I begged for this horrible reality to move far beyond the reaches of my mind. I was unsuccessful, remaining stationary, choosing to turn off the pain. It had become habit now and it was as automatic as turning off a light switch.

How I motivated myself to scramble out of the bin once my hands and legs were ripped from their bondage by their transgressor is beyond me. I was stiff and sore and walked with an uneven gait. The feeling in my stomach was a stabbing, strong and steady ache. I had been violated again but I did not dwell on it. I went outside, found my favourite spot and lay in the bushes, pulling myself together in a fetal position with my hands wrapped around my knees. I held on tightly, trying to push out the pain inside my soul.

There was a deep redness on my arms and legs. It was like I was trying to rip the shame from my body. My eyes were squeezed shut so tightly it hurt. The pressure wasn't helping, though. I was becoming more and more disturbed. It was when I heard the words, "Only babies cry" in my mind that a trace of a tear fell down my cheek. It could have so quickly become a torrent but I stopped it dead. I inhaled slowly, trying to match the denial of my tear to my shaky heart.

I listened to the birds singing softly in the trees. I opened my eyes just a crack to see if the world was still there. I saw butterflies fluttering, bugs digging their way into the soft mud. The leaves on the trees and the tall grasses waved back and forth, reminding me that not all of life was dark and cold. Calmness came over me like the soft, gentle breeze on my face. I floated along with it, unaware of myself. I had once again stopped the confusion, the crazed reality in which I lived.

AUNTIE BETH'S

I was pedaling down the road as fast as I could. My little legs were a blur of activity. The breeze felt good on my face and it was fun to ride around the potholes with the expertise that only a twelve-year-old possessed. The night's rain had made just enough moisture in the holes for a pleasant splash. Mother could be depended on to wash the dirty splatters out of my pants later. For now I was content to pedal on.

As I turned the corner into my uncle and aunt's yard, I could hear Laddie and Lassie barking their welcome. I called out to them and the two big collies came close, wagging their tails in a friendly hello. I half fell, half jumped off my bike and bent down to pet them in all their furry glory. Although my joy at seeing them was great, I knew that when I went up to the farm house door and knocked, my welcome would be even greater.

Sure enough, as soon as I was almost to the door, there was a tug on the door from the other side and there stood my aunt. A smile the size of a half moon spread across her face. If I could have seen my face, I'm sure my grin would have been twice the size. I knew the drill and went directly down the rickety basement steps. Everything was ready and I went to work without a word.

I found the egg baskets in their usual place. Grabbing the handle of the wire basket and taking the first delicate egg out, I put it in its slot. Then I watched with wonder as the egg came out the correct trough, extra small, small, medium and large. Sometimes the eggs where so small I kept them separate from the others. These would be eaten for breakfast by my aunt and uncle. Once the troughs were full I would begin to put them in big grey crates, stacking them one on top of the other. My aunt Beth was working right alongside me. We were a team. We moved in sync with each other, never having to say a word. I loved my aunt Beth and she loved me. Nothing could ever change that.

Once our task was complete, I would run up those same rickety stairs in anticipation of what was coming next. The smell in the air was a mixture of liniments and ointments and fresh baking. It was glorious. I lurched to a stop and peeked around the corner into the kitchen. My eyes slowly rose upwards to see the tabletop. Although I knew exactly what I would see, the thrill and anticipation never lessened. Aunt Beth rubbed my head from behind. I glanced up at her for the O.K. As she nodded her head I ran and jumped up onto my favourite old wooden chair. She sat across from me, her hands on her chin.

It was oatmeal chocolate chip cookies today. I looked at them longingly, but not for too long. My hands were itchy, my mind dreamily thinking about the warm, soft, melted chocolate that would soon be in my watering mouth. As I remember, those cookies were gone just like that. To complete the look, I added a milk moustache to the smears of chocolate on my face. My auntie was smiling to herself and she handed me a napkin so we could get on with the next step of our hallowed activities.

The board was ready and waiting on the table. I pulled it towards me, relishing the colourful pictures. Then, the game of Snakes and Ladders began. Auntie always let me go first. Together we were lost in the strategy of the game, unable to think of anything else, giggling at each move we made.

I lived for these times but dreaded the phone call which came all too soon. It was time for supper, time to go back home. Everything moved slowly then. I slowly tied my laces, spent extra time with the dogs and waited for my uncle Ted to come out of the chicken barns. He smelled awful but it was good to see him. We waved to each other as I slowly got on my bike.

The ride home was slow and methodical. I stayed away from the puddles and ruts on the way home so as not to anger Mother with my dirty pants. I drove on the yard; it was devoid of people. Walking inside I smelled supper on the table. I sat down in silence, gobbled down the food and moved through the rest of the evening without a word.

Later that night, in my room, I sat on the edge of the bed looking down at the floor. Rocking my body back and forth was soothing. It was comforting to feel the soft and real pressure of the movement, the movement that told me I was still alive. I was not dead. I liked being alone. Alone brought safety, it meant that I did not have to face the torment of relationship. Of crossing someone's path, of dealing with the uncomfortable struggle and strain of standing before someone, unheard and unwanted. I tried to dislodge myself from my reverie but I was paralyzed, paralyzed by fear. Maybe, just maybe if I sat all alone on the bed nobody would find me. Nobody would hear me. My thoughts became unbearable; the rocking grew worse. It was deep and long now. I felt my face wet with tears, something I had taught myself long ago not to feel, not to do. I turned off the tap as quickly as it had come. Numbness passed over me, bringing the blessed relief of denial. I truly was safe here alone in my room, all alone in my room.

As much as I felt guilty for feeling it, I really hated everything about home. The promise of racing down the road to my Aunt Beth's brought joy and elation to my little heart. Coming back from my auntie's left an awkward void. I felt grace at Aunt Beth's, a sense of relief. There was no second-guessing what she felt about you or what she was going to do to you. You could live in a harmony that came from just being with someone, no pretense involved. There wasn't really anything expected of you and what there was, you were glad to give. It was manageable.

Walking through the door of my home created extreme anxiety. The unknown deadlines, the scrambling to obey when you didn't know what the actual order would be. All the second guessing left constant commotion in the minds of four trapped souls, trying not to get in any trouble. The threat was very real. I was left feeling like a tiny black ant on a hill, all the other ants scurrying over each other with seemingly no purpose. A giant foot was standing over the hill menacingly, waiting to stomp out delicate life. Basic survival instincts kicked in, but with no apparent direction, scurrying away from all sense of fear. Honestly, I much preferred my Aunt Beth's. There I could breathe solid, sane breaths.

Not even sleep gave me relief from my terror. In my dreams, I experienced the day's events over and over. Running, I was running and running, tears streaming down my face. No matter how hard I tried to make them stop, they rained down harder and harder. They wouldn't stop.

A blurry path lay before me. I stumbled over the uneven ground in fear for my life. I was all alone. There was no one there to hold a hand, to provide comfort. The wind blew strong; I could not run against it. There was something behind me, but every time I turned my head, it disappeared. I knew it was there. I heard it. I heard it grunting and groaning, nothing could slow it down. It felt as though it was right on top of me now. It was out to get me and I knew it would. I would just have to run harder. By now, I was panting and out of breath. My side ached horribly, but I pushed on.

I played a game in my mind. I decided I was running towards a brilliant light. It meant safety. Maybe I could find my favourite hiding place in the hedge. I would be there soon, very soon I decided, and then this whole experience would stop its incessant madness. I concentrated on the soft, tiny willow buds, so delicate to the hand.

Would safety reign when I touched those bushes?

I took another chance and quickly drew a glance behind me. Still, I could see nothing, but that did not stop my uneasiness. I grew frantic. What if I fell, and gave my opponent the upper hand in attacking me with his strength, his might? I shuddered at the thought. I must keep moving grabbing hold of the element of time. If only I could disappear, become invisible. I was sure if only I wished it hard enough it would become true. I imagined myself the assistant to a magician, behind the curtain for a second, and then vanished to a world far away.

I waited, but nothing happened. I was still there and it was still behind me. I grew weary, tired of the whole game. I was losing the strength to go on.

I jerked into an upright position. I was not running nor being chased but sitting up in my creaky, old bed. I knew I had been crying out. My breathing was rapid, I was hyperventilating. I looked through the dark to make sure it was gone. My fear had taken over and I had to get control. I slowly evened out my breathing, finally understanding that it had just been a dream. It was the same nightmare I had had almost every night, forever. I was still petrified as I lay back down, my heart racing.

My eyes grew vacant. I couldn't help but stare clear across the room. As far as I knew, there was nothing at the other end of the dark tunnel that enshrouded me. Feelings divorced from reality, I accepted the fear as a part of my being. There wasn't anything to turn to. I accepted the dark chasm unwillingly. I groped in my mind for some sense of hope, but my senses betrayed me. I was lost. I tried to figure out the bitter truth of what had happened. In all honesty, I didn't really want to know. It was a fine art to keep the memories as far away as possible, and that's where I wanted them to stay.

"Fear is not a disease of the body; fear kills the soul."

Mahatma Gandhi

PLOTTED AGAINST

I was torn. I wanted to make some sense out of what was going to happen next, in this room. Once I had thoroughly exhausted all my options in my mind I realized my ill fate. I knew that I was to sit on the bed obligingly. I did not want to see or know what was coming next. For the entire procedure, I squished my eyes shut as tight as they would go. My body tensed, my shoulders sagged. I covered my eyes with my hands.

The routine never varied from its path. Inside, I had nothing more than a longing for peace and relief. But I knew my head would be forced down in a swirl. I knew his hair would smell of farm and dirt. I knew my mouth would be pushed around, spinning like a bottle top. And I knew I could not allow the retching I felt in my soul to rise up.

The only way to get through this sadistic venture was to remain strong and solid on the outside. It was much easier with my eyes shut and my soul shut down. Going somewhere else, somewhere clean and pure, somewhere far away into the hot sun where warmth created fake wholeness.

My thoughts were jerked back to reality as darkness itself knelt over me. It wasn't the first time I had seen it pulled out of his pants, but every time it happened again, it made my stomach sick and the promise of vomit was soon to follow. I had been brainwashed into never allowing my true feelings to show. I swallowed my knee-jerk response, readying myself for what was to follow. Reluctantly, I opened my mouth a crack. A smile rested on him as though this was a most wondrous event. As he squeezed it between the crack in my mouth, I forced my head to remain straight and steady. Closing my eyes, I tried to imagine some cleansing reality; this had no effect on the horror of my present world.

Shove after shove brought a revolting squirt of smelly, sticky juice. My gag reflex came on strong and I began to heave. A firm hand was placed on my head. I knew this was my cue to swallow the slimy substance down. It would soon become a part of my body, scarring me forever. By sheer force of will, I constricted my throat and gulped in the jelly-like substance. A trickle of urine escaped from a gruesome body and his hands came down on me even more forcefully.

While he savoured each movement he made; in and out, in and out, I cried out silently in my mind for redemption. I did not even know what it was that I really wanted, except at the very least, to be released from this cruel joke. The guilt and the shame took hold fiercely every time. I pondered what I had done to deserve this torture. My mind tried desperately to cling to some sense of sanity, but I found none. The only freedom was in denial and there was no choice but to take hold of it, strong and unwavering. I began to dream, to soar above the clouds into a magic kingdom made only for me, a kingdom where I was touched by good and good alone. In the real world, I was tied up on a creaky bed, bound in soul darkness, rejected by my small world, left to the vices of madness.

Although the small details do not come easy, the sinking feeling of desperation was strong. I hoped that God's protection was great but I did not know how many times I could go through this sickening ritual before cracking in two. I peeked beyond the mound of hair and saw the same old dirty shirt and narrow jeans filled with grease. The smell was overwhelming. His dirty brown hair fell over his eyes, dandruff falling gently with each raw movement.

The depraved motion was broken occasionally by groans of satisfaction. I cried out inwardly. There was no denying this sick past time. It was all too real. The smell of his dripping sweat met my senses with an unpleasant jolt.

I obediently climbed far under the covers. The avoidance and darkness brought calmness to my soul, surreal as it was. Blocking out the actions of this man felt right. This was the biggest family secret there was and I had no choice but to enter into it.

Horrible sounds emanated from his body for some time. It sounded like a kind of wild animal calling out to creation. I never figured out how the rest of the family could not hear these bizarre noises and come to my rescue. But help never came and I remained the object of some insufferable experiment. The family secret lived on perpetually. My choice was crushed; my life went on and with it, its undeniable loss of innocence, abuse running rampant.

I cannot describe the breaking away from self, although I know I mastered it very well. It was my only form of self-protection. Separating myself from the sickening touch of his groping and pushing created an alternate reality which was bearable.

There was a saccharin, sweet kindness that emanated from him for a while after these episodes. He lay on one side of me when he was through whispering the key importance of the secret. He told me how special I was and how special these times were. I kept my head under the covers so he could not see my repulsion at what he had made me do. This secret love he declared echoed in the hollows of the room. Was I to delight in this revelation or turn off all longing to be loved by this man?

I imagined myself playing with my dolls, I basked in the sunshine, I played with my dog and created a thousand more adventures for myself as I lay in that horrible twin bed listening to his offering of renewed love.

HOLLOW

Empty, alone I stand with nothing to offer

Imperfect, never victorious, unloving

With strange fears

Scared, timid, Unsure of my future

Worried, Misunderstood, Confused

Tired of trying, Thinking, Frustrated

Yet with the knowledge, yet with the knowledge stored within me

Of a God who promises to accept me exactly as I am

A BARN ROOF

We lived on the prairies where, not only was old Mister Wind almost always blowing, but where each year winter always came with a white furious blast. As odd as it was, I lived for the drifts that grew tall and hard. It was a challenge to see how far I could go without sinking down into them and getting a boot full of snow. Of course we were well armored in our snowsuits, toques, scarves and mitts, each of them mismatched and colourful. The only skin to be seen was a small slit for the eyes, which was usually so frosted up, you could barely see. Ice crystals would attach themselves to your eyelashes and blinking didn't really take care of the problem. The only way to get rid of the frost was to sit by the heater in the inviting warmth of the farm house.

One winter day I was contentedly trudging through the snow with Andy behind me, anticipating the ride of a lifetime. We each had a dark blue snow carpet in hand. They were ripped and chewed up on the sides but if you sat on them just right, none of that mattered. We began the ascent to the top of the barn roof, making a path for the next time we would go up. Our boots sank deep into to the snow each time and we laughed as we got boot full after boot full.

As we reached the top the view was wondrous. The view from the dilapidated barn roof brought a whole new meaning to the prairies being flat. You could see for miles and miles around. The world was a sparkling, snowy white in the bright sunshine. The sun dogs where especially brilliant today, creating an even more spectacular sight.

I breathed in and out deeply behind my scarf, causing steam to rise up out of the top of it, warming my face like a sauna. I saw Andy getting ready for the long descent and joined him as quickly as I could. After all, who could let her little brother beat her down the hill on the first run of the season? I had to be the first one; it was only right. I jumped onto the carpet sliding this way and that, trying to get into the proper position. A hard crust on the snow made the challenge even greater, the slippery surface fighting against any kind of stability. I planted my feet firmly on either side of the carpet and finally got my bearings. My eyes surveyed the steep decline off of the pig barn, mapping out the best path. Bumps and then hollows met my eye. It would be best to hit them dead on.

Finally I was ready to go. Off I went, with Andy following a close second. The anticipation was palpable. The ride started out slowly, but by pushing the carpet along with my hands and feet, I was soon moving swiftly along the drifting snow. The first bump made screams fly out of my mouth and I could hear Andy crying out with glee a few seconds behind. I whirled around in a complete circle, losing all control. Falling off my perch I rolled the rest of the way down the hill, laughing to my heart's content. It didn't get better than this on a cold wintry day.

Flat on my back, I lay looking up at the sky, thanking God that there were good days too. I watched as my brother flew the rest of the way down. He made it unscathed to the bottom, laughing his head off as he saw me flat on my back in the snow. We both knew he had won after all.

The rest of the afternoon went on in the same manner. Either we were flying down the roof or trudging up it. We never grew tired of the routine. We only went home when it grew dark at four o'clock. Life was rich.

FELINES

"If we have no peace, it is because we have forgotten that we belong to each other."

Mother Teresa

I loved my cats to pieces, literally; Black Paws, Gray Paws, Blackie, amazingly original names. But then again, we had twenty-one cats one spring, all either grey or black. I would practically squish them to death as I held them in my arms. We owned the grand matriarch of all cats. Beauty was her name. She was proud and cold except for when she chose to be otherwise. She would purr and rub herself up against your leg with her dirty fur. Her dirt came from rolling around in the garden, but it did not take much to rub the black specks away. She had kittens every spring and sometimes in the fall. She usually hid them up in the rafters of the old barn, attentively caring for them. If you touched them and she found any human scent on them, she would move them. Sometimes she hid them so well, no one could find them. These kittens would become wild unless, with a lot of patience, they were enticed to come close. A piece of leftover chicken would usually do the trick, drawing them in with its delicious smell. Beauty was Joy's cat and she lived the longest of all our cats.

I think cats were one of the ways I found a calmness inside. Just caring for them gave me a good feeling, a feeling that I was doing something good and right.

I will never forget one spring when a stray cat showed up on our yard. Her belly was full of little ones, just waiting to pop out. I fed her faithfully awaiting the arrival of her kittens. I was extremely excited. Finally, one day, she had four small baby kittens. I made them a home of old rags in the little shed at the back of the house. The gray striped cat that brought these tiny creatures into the world was well fed as her squirmy little kittens drank from her with eager mouths. I never touched the kittens because I was sure the Mother would take them away. The Mother cat often went hunting, bringing back assorted goodies for her children. They mewed and twisted their heads toward the sound of her paws, anticipating the newfound delicacies. Her hunting excursions took her further and further away until one warm spring day she did not return.

The grey fur balls mewed and mewed for their Mother to no avail, so I decided to become a surrogate. I asked Mother for a clean rubber glove. It was made of thick latex and was bright yellow. I then proceeded to poke holes in the finger tips, squishing them to make sure the air came through. I asked Mother for some creamy milk from our dairy cow, Daisy. We milked her each day for our own drinking pleasure. I slowly poured the milk into the glove while holding the tips shut. I was sure that would do the trick. I walked out to the shed carefully, not wanting to spill even a drop of the special formula. There were four fingers and four kittens so it should work out just right. They certainly did not come rushing towards me as if I was their Mother. I carefully took them one by one and forced the tip of the glove into each tiny mouth. Nothing, they were not drinking. I began to panic. What would I do now?

I went back into the house and told Mother my terrible tale. She smiled and then laughed aloud. I did not take kindly to that. How could she laugh when my kittens where going to starve to death. She took the milk-filled glove, went to the cupboard, dumped the creamy milk into a bowl and added white sugar. Then she stirred it and warmed it in the microwave. She returned the milk to me and I returned to the kittens to try again.

This time, although it was clumsy and awkward for them, they did their best to retain as much of the sweet liquid as they could. Milk dribbled down their tiny faces. They looked adorable. How could their Mother abandon them? I nursed those kittens for weeks on end, in the morning before school, after school, and in the evening before I went to bed. Eventually I added some mashed-up gruel when I thought they could handle solid foods. They had become my babies and I loved them. They were truly all mine.

STUCK IN THE MUD

It was a warm and wonderfully bright spring day. We had all eaten breakfast, except for Andy, who was still sound asleep in bed, and now everybody was up to something.

Father was in his blessed shed deciding what to fix next. It was between the harrows and the tractor, but he needed a part for it. He was antsy to get started and taking the time to drive twenty or so miles there and back to the store was just too big of an inconvenience. So he chose the harrows. Every spring it was the same thing. It was as if the blood in Father's veins was super-charged. His focus was intense, his motivation sure. His only thought was to get his equipment ready to get out on the land, claiming ownership to each clump of dirt.

Joy was busy with her assigned tasks for the morning. She never veered from doing her chores the proper way. She insisted that everything had to be put in its place. Sometimes she sulked about my willy-nilly ways but the way I figured no one was making her do anything. She chose to create all this regimented organization for herself, so why cry to Mother about my nonchalant attitude? She made work for herself. I couldn't help it if I knew how to get out of it.

Keith and I were left at the table with Mother. We had only begged and pleaded with her for the last several weeks to be able to go out into the acres of field barefooted. No matter what antics we used, what force we applied, she was impenetrable. "You'll catch your death of cold," she decided. Then she would reminisce about her years of experience with the prairie muck. She became completely convinced my brother and I would sink down into the earth, never to rise to see the light of day again. Try as we might to persuade her otherwise, she remained unswerving.

Still, the muck and the mire were calling out to my brother and me. It was one of the few times Keith and I agreed on anything. It was begging us to let go of all inhibitions and join nature as one unified creation. How could Mother dampen our dreams, our dreams of becoming one, one with the mud? Today as we asked, something was distinctly different. It was almost as though she was toying with us. Underneath her stern exterior, something was smiling. Someone was giggling away like a little girl playing a wild game of hide and seek. It was almost as though she had decided that today was the day we would get our wish, our dream would come true. And sure enough, after a good half hour of twisting our little child minds around, she said we could go. Just like that. It all seemed so easy now that the taunting was over.

We ran upstairs, donning torn shorts and t-shirts. They appeared more like rags than anything. Our hearts were beating a mile a minute and our heads were in a whirl.

Keith outran me by far but I didn't care because I knew I would get there sooner or later. Mother said we had to help each other in the muck, but with our relationship the way it was, we couldn't bear to get close enough to touch. If one of us wobbled, the other one pushed gently on the other's arm or shoulder. That was as close as we got to helping each other. It didn't really matter anyway, because the minute we got into the field, we began to sink down deep into the black muck. It was just as Mother had predicted.

The trick was to hop along the surface of the wet dirt with great agility as quickly as possible. Otherwise, your feet would get sucked down, deeper and deeper into the hazardous black clay. When that happened, that was it. The loud sucking sound of trying to pull out one foot and then the other could be heard across the prairie landscape. It sounded like someone had just hit the end of a very thick milkshake, only ten times as loud. Sometimes we would laugh so hard our bottoms would plop into the mushy clay, and then we would be really stuck.

It seemed like we had been forging on forever, but when we looked back we saw that we had come only a few feet. The spring rains had created an uncontrollable monster out of the clay and we were the unkempt, muddied victims. We looked a sight for sore eyes and felt a sight worse. We were growing tired of trying to push our way through this unstoppable force. After what seemed forever, we slowly plodded our way back to safety. Since we were filthy to the core, we took the opportunity to war against each other with mighty onslaughts of the black, watery clumps of dirt. Pushing each other down and slapping globs of mud everywhere brought forth fits of laughter from our beings. This was the life. We knew we would pay for it when we arrived back home but for now, this vortex of joy was all that mattered.

When we could no longer see each other's faces, we decided to return on our long journey home. We walked past the row of bushes that surrounded the farmhouse. We walked past the small machine shed where the old machinery lay in disarray on the somewhat scrubbed floor; the garden plot that Father had just tilled, getting it ready for planting. Then we marched up the final stretch of driveway, past the huge rocks on either side.

Mother sat on the porch with a stern look on her face as if to say, "You are not coming in the house looking like that." She said not a word but pointed to the outside garden hose. It was hooked up to the pond water. Now the pond water was freezing cold. Actually, it was beyond cold, reaching into frigid. Did she really expect us to use that water to wash with? I looked clearly at her, drawing the truth out of those eyes of hers.

Without a word being spoken, Keith and I knew she was serious. Suddenly the warm spring day became ridiculously cold. We started with our hands, gingerly pouring the water over them to wash the black away. Shivers of delight turned to shivers of frozen ice, bubbling up on the skin, bright pink and then brighter red. There was no doubt about it, we wouldn't ask again next year. But there was also no doubt about this—the wait had been well worth it.

A PRAIRIE GARDEN

"The most authentic thing about us is our capacity to create, to overcome, to endure, to transform, to love and to be greater than our suffering."

Ben Okri

Weeding the garden was a regular chore for my sister and me throughout the whole summer. Mother planted a massive garden each year. The only way you could see the end of the hearty crop was by the tall row of corn far in the distance. She had a way with her plants. They flourished under her care. For her, the business of gardening was cathartic. It brought energy and strength to her soul. I suppose she expected the same spirit to come out in her daughters and although I loved watching the garden grow, I cannot say I loved tending to it.

Just the same, we each had our rows of vegetables to weed laboriously each week, sometimes twice because of the rain. It was easier to weed vegetables like beans and peas which grew straight up toward the light, making the weeds easy to find. Cucumbers twisted down along the ground, scattering themselves around on vines, making the weeds harder to find. My sister got the job of lifting up each plant and looking underneath for any sign of the annoying little weeds.

I often took more breaks than I did work. I grew weary of the boring task Mother had given me so I decided to dig for worms instead. They were long, mushy, and divided into a million sections. They felt good in my hands. It was somewhat intriguing to stretch them as far as I could without ripping them in two. I heard somewhere that it didn't matter if they got all ripped up because they could regenerate themselves into even more worms. That was a bizarre thought.

Joy was never very happy with me. She accused me of quitting work whenever Mother left to do something else. I shrugged my shoulders; the only thing that I could see was that she took her responsibilities far too seriously. There were better things to do with the spare time here on earth than to labour for someone else.

She made her bed meticulously. She laid out her clothes every night. She was always helpful and mostly polite. She never crossed anyone and always pleased everyone. These had always been some of the differences between us. I ran away from work and she ran towards it and embraced it. This was beyond my comprehension. Why wouldn't I or anyone get away with as much as they possibly could? As far as I was concerned, she could go her way and I would go mine.

I grew bored of this task involving the dividing of the worms as well and decided to take a real rest. I lay down carefully, so as not to damage the thriving green pea plants. Now I was face to face with the sun. I closed my eyes dreamily reflecting on my small life. In the day light, all was at rest. What could be more soothing than lying down in the sun on a warm, summery day?

Feeling the warmth of the black dirt on my skin, I looked up into the sunny sky and watched the soft, fluffy clouds pass by. I began to name them one by one. The shapes were phenomenal. There were animals big and small, ships, angels and everything under the sun. They passed by, all dream-like, bringing warmth and comfort.

This did not last long; mixed up thoughts stepped into my mind. The terror that had overcome me in the basement the past few days left me feeling weary and tired. I preferred to dwell on the world around me. The summer breeze blowing gently across my face brought a calming relief. This world of nature and wonder was where I belonged. Looking at the cold, dark recesses of my mind gave me the chills. It shattered the beauty of my God-given world. Refusing to dwell on the blackness within I chose light and wholeness instead. I smiled at the day, drinking in the sights and sounds. I would choose the nearness of nature as my guide. Nothing could get in my way then.

STAMPEDING ALONG

The rooster had not even let out his shrill call for the day yet when Father arose from his bed we knew it was Stampede time. He threw on his usual sagging jeans and a brightly checkered shirt to match. Although he tried to shut the bedroom door quietly on his way out, a hollow thud could be heard throughout the house. His pace was dramatic as he walked from window to window. The east showed little but the rising sun. He moved to the west window. It stood narrow and tall next to the piano. He sat for a moment on the antique piano bench and looked deeply into the horizon. It looked like a good and proper sky, pure and blue, but he couldn't be sure.

A row of bushes obscured his view. He jumped off the squeaky, round seat and headed for the door. He had to get outside where he could see the sky better. Pulling on his worn work boots, he opened the outside door to the clanging of the bell, and then took the liberty of slamming the door behind him. He took in a breath of fresh air while the rest of us groaned and rolled over back to the comfort of our warm blankets, settling in to wait for the next very broad hint from Father.

My dog Dusty rose from his house under the kitchen window beside the porch. He stretched his long body and let out a tired, morning "Arg." He sauntered over to Father, less than enthusiastically, for his perfunctory pat on the head. He got the extra treatment today of a well-deserved rub behind the ears and a "Come on, let's go." Dusty was happy to accompany Father around the corner of the house and they meandered happily through a trail in the trees. It was summer so the leaves were lush and the insects plentiful. They let off a playful buzz. Father heard and saw none of it. He was determined to greet the horizon with all the enthusiasm he had. Once on the other side of the bushes, he repeated the process of checking the weather from the west. He was pleased. It was going to be a bright, sunny day.

He couldn't resist stooping down, grabbing one tender shoot of golden wheat in his weathered hand, breaking off the head from the stalk and rolling it around and around in his hands. He was deeply satisfied that this was going to be a bumper crop. Smiling at the process of time and his deep dedication to the land, he turned on his heel and walked steadily back to the little farm house with Dusty at his side. All was right with the world.

He turned the corner to the cement porch, its yellow roof a beacon to all who drove on the yard. The bumpy, gravel road led right up to its flashy stardom. (I always hated that yellow roof). It was like a sea of waves, bright yellow and full of dirt and leaves. Every rain meant a plethora of muck would come down off the edge, along with the clean, refreshing rain. Sitting down on the deacon's bench, he rubbed Dusty behind the ears and proudly looked around his empire. There were too many metal bins, tanks and implements to count. He felt like a king, sitting there on that bench. Dusty had now graduated up into his lap and was soaking up honest and pure affection.

Father sat still as long as he could, which was never very long for him. Then he heard the sounds he had been waiting for. The dark, strong coffee was brewing and the bacon began sizzling in the pan. This was his long-awaited cue to move towards the squeaky door, and not to forget to take off his muddy boots OUTSIDE. He had forgotten so many times, I still remember the huge commotion that mistake cost us all. Once a lesson learnt, always a lesson learnt?

Mother was cracking the fresh eggs into the cast iron skillet when Father appeared in the kitchen doorway. No words were spoken, no hugs exchanged. He simply sat down in HIS chair and drew two long-lived green Corelle cups from the cupboard above him.

He waited patiently, toes tapping and legs shaking, as the coffee dripped with intolerable slowness into its pot. He watched Mother work over the hot stove, juggling the bacon, eggs, and toast. The bacon was crispy, the eggs over easy and the homemade bread toasted and buttered to within an inch of its life.

Mother's best meal was breakfast. Eventually we children meandered down the narrow stairway, greeted by the fragrant smell. We all knew our places in the cramped kitchen and munched on toast while Mother went back to work at the hot stove on what was turning out to be a very hot day. We could never get away from the evangelical reading of the Daily Bread. So I watched the orioles and finches, bright with colour, while Father droned on.

My sister and I were cleaning up when it dawned on me that it was Stampede Day. The more I thought about it, the clumsier I got. I juggled the dishes as they passed through my hands to their fate below. At times, my quick morning reflexes caught the antique, green Corelle plates and, at other times, they fell to the floor. My sister rolled her eyes and proceeded with her duty of putting them in the dishwasher.

It being Saturday and all, the house had to be gone through to some degree. We had to do all our routine chores on Saturday because Sunday was church. Father mostly just drove around, stopping to see how his crops were doing. The swather and combine were not out in the field yet, but Father was dreaming of being out there anyway. Eventually he came back to the house to see if it was time to go. The sweeping and vacuuming and the cleaning of the kitchen were most important to Mother, and of course I am sure she felt a slight glee in her heart, for she was in control for once.

Of course, the men all sat in the living room and read, knowing they could not dissuade Mother from disinfecting her home before we went. The boys were antsy and frustrated, and Father was just plain impatient. He never sat in his chair for long. He paced from window to window in long strides trying to hasten the process. Looking out the west window to check for rain and pacing the length of the living room where high on his check list of annoying things to do. He finally found something useful to do and picking up his harmonica to play a few tunes for us. He was considerably good at the old instrument and we all felt the warmth of his love for music.

Finally Mother decided that enough of cleaning had been done for the day and announced it was time to march to the tune of a different drum, stampede day had arrived. The pitter-patter of four sets of feet could be heard, each trying to get the best spot in the famous white Mercury Grand Marquis, with its smooth, red velvet seats on the inside. It was kept scrupulously clean, inside and out. My seat was in the back, on the bump in the middle. The bump was a folding arm for when only two people sat and dwelt in harmony together. I had no choice but to lean one way or the other, creating conflict between brother and sister. "Don't touch me." "You stink." A scoundrel came across my face or my sister's face became par for the course. I had touched her arm or elbow and she was undignified. How could I help it if the road was bumpy? The dust flew up from the gravel road that wound along steadily. Instead of using the air conditioning, we kept the windows open in the back of the car. That saved on gas, but caused no end of frustration for me and my siblings.

There was a big bridge that brought us into Morris. I loved the smell, the swift current of the river; in spots there was even white water. It also meant the end of the journey. It was a real town once you passed over the bridge. Gas stations, restaurants, grocery stores and other buildings seemed like huge estates. After all, our small town of 52 had a little store, a Co-op, a school and the grain elevators which, of course, were the landmark. This was spectacular compared to that. We drove slowly down the highway although we were racing in our hearts. The cars were moving at a snail's pace. The whole world had come to the Stampede. Finally, after 30 minutes of dust, exasperation, and bumpy roads we arrived in great style at the fairgrounds. They were already bustling with enthusiastic, western rodeo types. We could hear the screams from the fair rides echoing from the Tilt-a-Whirl, the Swing and even the kiddie rides.

After 10 minutes of wonder, driving through the town, we pulled up to the stampede gate. A smiling, overly enthusiastic ticket-taker told Father what he needed for tickets. Our minds raced wildly, chanting "Fair rides, fair rides." There were no secrets given away about what kind of tickets had been purchased, despite our keenly attentive ears.

Next came parking; it was an eternal pain. The parking lot was made up of a green, bumpy field that had been freshly mowed. Father drove slowly and carefully along row after row already filled to capacity with cars. He did not want to wreck his new FORD GRAND MARQUIS. Finally he found a place and we landed without incident in a spot that cradled me in brother's lap as we turned sharply on the bumpy, grassy field. Keith was less than pleased and made a quick escape out the door. I then fell down in a ridiculous, twisted state. We had finally arrived at the stampede.

Walking to the gate as a family proved a pleasant experience. We were all so excited that our usual bickering and shoving stopped. In those days, we always started out with Mother, my sister (this did not suit her at all) and I. Mother and I liked looking at the same exhibits, but my sister was up for more excitement. With valuable money from Father in our dirty little palms, the boys tore off toward the livestock to see the bucking broncos and prize-winning bulls.

Right in the center of this mass of people, there was a market. The kitchen sink wasn't there, but cotton candy, ice cream and homemade baked goods all lined up together to make my mouth water. Cowboy hats, necklaces, rings, pottery, even today's newspapers all lined the cement avenue. The potato chip and popcorn vendors were all yelling, "Ge-e-e-et your popcorn here." They were doing pretty well with their wares, especially the drinks, on such a hot day.

Next we walked to a little barn. The first part consisted of a petting zoo. I knelt down beside a brown and white-patched goat. I petted his back; he was very warm and fuzzy. I loved the look in his clear blue eyes; kind and chuckling, it was almost like he knew a secret I didn't. He nuzzled my face and then with his little goat face up in the air he walked away. It was time to go on to the next stall, a brightly coloured pink pig. She lay on her side, staring into space, as her five little piglets suckled on her teats. They grunted and slopped all over their mama, squirming around in between each other like the happiest of mammals. There were oh! So many different species, all of them wonderful to behold, overwhelming me as my eye met theirs. Bantams and their baby chicks, white chickens, donkeys the size of a dog six hands high and lots of dust and straw to stir up my allergies.

In the back part of the smelly barn, there were exhibits upon exhibits, all under glass. There was everything there from penmanship to arts and crafts, science projects and paintings. I wandered around looking for anything from my school and happened upon a piece recognizing honour for…I read the parchment, getting to the bottom. The story sounded acutely familiar. I was nothing but shocked, for my name was on the bottom, right there in black and white. I had won first place in a writing and penmanship contest. That was completely crazy. I thought my writing was a disaster.

My head did not swell, nor my eyes take in the beauty of the prize; I had too little self-esteem to appreciate the school prize and the teacher's pride. Besides, I knew there would be no admiring comments from the family, even though I had won two or three awards for penmanship and writing over the years. They must have passed by the exhibit with no intention of letting me know how well I had done. It confused me as a recurring fact of life.

We all met at the picnic tables for lunch. Running to save a table out of the sun, we all smacked into each other with a gigantic thud. We sat on top of the table, watching the festivities around us. Flies swarmed on everyone and everyone waved at them in horrid defeat. They buzzed in your ears and eyes until running and screaming was your only option. My older brother could catch them in his hand and squish their lives, such as they were, to death. This was not Mother's favourite part of the day. She sat at the edge of the bench with her head in her hands. Drops of sweat were evident on her upper lip, a pitiful picture. Then she noticed Father coming our way, weaving his way through the crowd, carrying a huge tray of the Stampede staple food, hamburgers--huge hamburgers with every kind of sauce on them. Father never asked what condiments we wanted; he just plastered the sauces as high as possible. The French fries were from another world, thick and covered with salt, a heart attack waiting to happen, but oh! so soft on the inside, then came the guzzling of Coke, Coke, and more Coke.

As Father wove his way to the picnic table, we all scampered down from the table top, fighting for the place closest to where Father would set the tray down. My two brothers always got there first, even if it meant flying over a body and pushing us girls out of their way. We chowed down like we had never eaten before. The thick sauces dripped and dropped on shirts, pants, floors and everything else that got in the way. After all, it didn't matter much; we were outside, and the masses all looked the same. After lunch we switched partners and promised to meet by the stadium for the finals and the best event.

My new partner was much more fun than the old. My younger brother and I raced off to the fair. This is where the money from Father came in handy. We arrived at the ticket booth and asked how many tickets we could get for our money. We had no clue of the way the exchange went, but I asked to keep a few dollars back just in case I wanted a souvenir. Looking up after bargaining with the ticket-taker, we could finally take in the beauty of the fair.

The bright, blue sky with its soft clouds moving slowly across the atmosphere and the bright red and yellow fair rides were astounding. A menagerie of metal machinery, well oiled, so the rides would stay together and run smoothly, assured us of the best time ever. We rode the ones with the shortest lines first, hoping the kids on the big rides would move on to something else. That never happened, so we had to stand in line for the more infamous rides. The Swing left many a small, impressionable child spewing lunch up over the side of his seat. The Grand Prix Race Cars left most riders bashed every which way, stopping, starting, screaming to their hearts' content. Most of the fair was like that and we went right along with it. Life was good, but the best was yet to come.

Tired from out long journey through the stampede maze we found seats on the hard wooden benches. The vendors were out in full force and the clown in the center of the ring renewed our energy with his wild tricks. My head was spinning for even though the chariot races were last on the program, they were first in my mind. First, the clown, he always came out twirling twirls and jumping into somersaults, making everyone laugh uproariously. His bright-coloured clothes, polka-dotted yellow and red shirt, the bright blue baggy pants to offset the hot orange, curly hair, all created the perfect introduction. Suddenly, a calf burst out of a gate, a calf roper and horse hot on its heels. The crazy clown ran the other way, trying to hide.

The first cowboy out on the floor was a calf roper. He started swirling his loop 'round and 'round up high in the air, waiting for just the right moment to lasso the helpless calf. The clown ran hither and thither, running away or towards the whole scenario until at last the cowboy had lassoed the calf in record time.

Although he was just a wacky old clown, he had a more important role than one would have thought. If the cowboy got into any sort of trouble, the clown was there to help get him out of it.

Wagon races, horse races (Mother's favourite), barrel racing were all next in line. Many screams and wails came from all over the stands but when the chariot riders came out, they received a standing ovation. The riders, standing on their chariots, were dressed in Roman armour. Holding the leather reigns in their hands, the horses were wild, stepping back and forth ready to fly away at any minute. The shiny metal shone in the sun and the feathers on their helmets blew in the mighty wind.

There were four beautiful horses, each of them lined up perfectly. The horses continued in readiness to push forward at their owners command. The gun went off, the horses' noses flared dramatically, then the reigns were let go on the horses' back, and off they went, some rearing up. The expected shout from the crowd cheering shot out like a gun shot. Every eye was on the horse and driver. The blowing dust was intolerable; every dedicated horse fan was caught between rubbing dust out of their eyes and squinting at the beautiful sight. Starting into the first corner, some of the dust dispersed, but it was harder to see from this distance.

So far they were all running neck and neck. The announcer was bellowing out the positions, a voice half-drowned out by audience participation. Still running in a dead heat, the horses began to turn the second corner. The drivers had a time and half trying to control the horses around the corner. One chariot in particular leaned well away from its horse on one wheel and into another chariot. Shouts arose in the anticipation of what could happen. In the end all righted themselves and chariot and driver ran smoothly along on two wheels. Around the last corner and the race was over. The well-muscled horses were frothing at the mouth, as the proud winner was announced and the night was over. We jumped up as fast as we could and ran for the car, trying not to be engulfed in the crowd, but the same smile was on all of our faces, the smile of victory.

STICKS AND STONES

There was no real give and take in my family, only the arbitrary authority of Father. He was the head of the household and nobody dared to cross his path. He was commander of his generational army and we were the obedient soldiers. I would not be lying in the sun on his watch. His unforgettable solution to disobedience was some form of severe, corporal punishment. Our relationship was mostly, "Do this, do that." Tasks were the primary focus.

One day, when I was busy weeding our acre of garden, I heard a troubling commotion. I sat up and saw big brother, Keith, across the yard close to the big shed. It was grey and had a sloped roof. There was a cement pad in front of it but inside it was a dirt floor. I never knew my older brother very well. But I did know he was sorely mistreated by Father.

Fear crept in as I watched Father tell Keith his next task. He was to fill the big red tractor with gasoline. It was time to go out to "the other land" and do some harrowing.

leaves falling   through the air

sunlight falling   down, down on me

thoughts

exploding

bringing

unexpected pain,

a longing

for truth,

for peace

and life

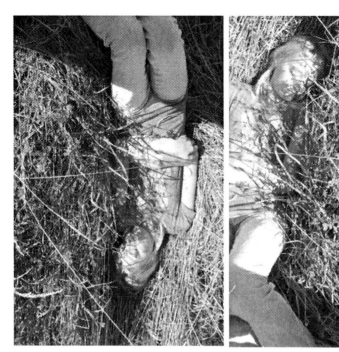

unworthy of such thoughts, I become invisible

become one with the world, death brings life

warmth to my soul, soft, glowing colors warm my mind

turning my back on evil, I will find the truth

in the hard places   forging head

higher I go to touch the sun, I forever journey on

The expression on Father's face was sour and demeaning. His voice grew loud. I could hear his harsh tone from across the big yard. Keith fell silent as his gaze fell to the ground. As far as I could see, Keith wasn't even kicking up a stink. He just stood immobile waiting, waiting. I watched closely to see if Father would raise his hand but today must have been a good day because Keith ran off as fast as he could to complete Father's task. I lay back down in the dirt, sighing with relief. Another crisis had been averted. There was a twinge of pain inside but with no one to tell, I decided to go back to my weeding. Feeling the dirt in my fingers was soothing. It helped me to forget and go on.

COLD AND CRACKED

"Part of every misery... is the misery's shadow: you don't merely suffer but keep on thinking that you suffer. I live each endless day in grief, and think about living in grief."

C.S. Lewis

Coming home from school meant fun and games with my younger brother, Andy. When it got too cold to go outside, we were relegated to the basement. It always smelled a little soggy down there. There was no drywall or anything, nothing to create a hint at beauty in the dismal atmosphere. It was grey and bleak. Sometimes the sewer backed up into it and then the smell was hideous.

Well, that was after we had flush toilets. In the old days we had a five gallon bucket which we used for our human waste. It was in the room where the tub was. I say this because you couldn't really call it a bathroom. It was a place where the bucket was situated, the tub was put and the ringer washer sat. The tub was a claw foot tub, as heavy as can be. And it was painted pink on the outside.

Whenever the "bucket" was full, my brother Keith would have to haul it up the creaky old stairs. Nobody in my family really took too much care in "how" they did their business so this was a hideous task. And you can just imagine how heavy a five gallon bucket of crap was. I hid around the corner of the basement stairs, careful not to get in the way. My nose was squeezed shut by my fingers, my mouth turned up in a big "Yuck," and one eye slightly open, wondering why there wasn't a lid for the twisted concoction inside the bucket. I watched as it sloshed back and forth, with Keith being careful not to spill anything over the edge. The smell was beyond this world. I admired Keith's strength, not only physically, but his stamina in putting up with all the crap, literally.

Despite the cold and the smell, the basement became our play place every winter. We were either shooed outside or downstairs. There was one free wall to bounce a ball against and Andy and I played 7-Up to our hearts' content. There were seven steps to this game; each set of bounces got harder and harder. One bounce on the wall, one on the floor and so on until it was one bounce on the wall, two on the floor and over the leg, then the final catch. We hardly ever made the seventh step but we sure had fun trying.

The little basement was almost too small for the sets in the game so there were occasional crashes into some item that had been left in the middle of the floor. The one good thing was that the floors and walls were cement. The red and blue rubber ball had excellent bouncing power because of the hard surface. Sometimes we would slam the ball down as hard as we could on the floor and see if we could get it to fly up and touch the ceiling. We would stand with our arms crossed, counting the number of bounces, before the ball would stop. Sometimes we got up to four bounces floor to ceiling. This was a major accomplishment and we would high five each other, hoot and holler, trying again.

It seemed that these small attempts at pleasure in my life were torn away from me in one way or another. This time it was by the heavy footsteps coming down the basement stairs. I cringed, and sank down, slumping my shoulders, turning off all emotion. Andy slunk away. I didn't blame him. There was nothing that could be done to save me from what was about to come.

A dark shadow came and stood over me, just standing, waiting. I could almost see the silent smirk written across his face, but I was too afraid to look up. It was better if I was submissive. There was less chance of bruising to my body and my spirit. I sunk to my knees and held out my hands. They were tied awkwardly around and round with harsh bailer twine. It ripped into my skin sometimes, causing blood to trickle down my arms. I was pulled roughly to my feet and pushed towards the pantry door. As the door opened, I was dragged along carelessly by my arm. I closed my eyes tight, squishing them tight, trying desperately to move myself into my safe place. It wasn't working; the intensity of the situation was just too much.

Most of the time I just dropped on the dirty floor and was left in the dark, but today something different was up. A new plan was being hatched. Before I knew it, I was thrown up and over a half wall into the potato bin. The potatoes were rotting and the smell of mold and a putrid stench rose up into my nostrils. I lay there like a caged animal. More twine was applied to my ankles to ensure my capture. It was bumpy and uncomfortable but more than that, totally humiliating. He didn't speak a word; silence reigned. When he was done wielding his power over me, he left the room, locking the door behind him.

Hog-tied and in the dark, I wished he had blindfolded me. This way I was tempted to open my eyes, only to realize I was alone in the darkness, all alone. All sense of time disappeared. There was nothing to do but wait, wait for a salvation that would never come. I always ended up tied and gagged. The musty smell of the basement became like home to me. Lying in the darkness and cold, feeling it seeping through my body and into my soul, entrenched me in a hopeless world. At first I tried to climb out of it but slowly became lost in it. My only strategy for destroying the darkness was the power of my mind. The dreams I clung to kept me alive.

THERE AGAIN

I was back there again. THERE was hard to define. All that I knew was that the nausea and blackness would come. I closed my eyes trying to envision something beautiful. I prayed hard and long. "God, take this from me." But I never really knew what "this" was. It was a hard cold knot in the pit of my stomach. It was a dizzying headache that wouldn't go away. It was the endless nightmare of running, sweat dripping down. I was too scared to look back. It was all these things and more. They devastated me, created havoc in my small life. Daytime had its empty spots. There were blanks that couldn't be found. They haunted me when I concentrated hard and tried to figure out what lurked in them. After a while, there were too many to count. I would give up my quest to try to make sense out of my life and simply forget, until they struck again, the cruelty of my day and the nightmares of the night.

The pain of my dark reality edged in. I fought to remain separate from it but despite all of my hard work of moving towards denial, my thoughts became unbearable all too soon. My breathing grew deep and long. There was a little quiver in my body. I felt my face; it was wet with tears but I tried to hold back the sobs. I did not want to get to the point of no return.

"We are all sentenced to solitary confinement inside our own skins, for life."

Tennessee Williams

"Of all tyrannies a tyranny sincerely exercised for the good of its victims may be the most oppressive."

C.S. Lewis

92

HOME SWEET HOME

"In the depths of winter, I finally learnt there was in me an invincible summer."

Albert Camus

The Klassens' was a pleasant place to be. I could go there, spending time away from the reality of the chaos I found in the house in which I lived. I could deny the disintegration of my own small life. They lived miles down a gravel road, but it never felt like long to get there. Bill was a truck driver. He drove all over Canada and the States. He was gone for long stretches of time, leaving May, his wife, to care for the family farm all on her own. Bill's brother lived with them. He was quiet and stuck to himself. Most of the time, we never even saw him. He would get a plate of steaming hot food at dinnertime and take it back to his room. I always admired him, in a way. He had the art of invisibility down to a science.

The Klassen house was cluttered with all sorts of good stuff. For one thing, there were trinkets galore. I am sure there was a china cabinet in every room displaying the many wonders May had collected over the years. There was the Royal Dalton collection, a collection of vases, of antiques and all sorts of little handmade treasures.

Mrs. Klassen had a kiln in her basement and she made beautiful plates, hand painted. She also made porcelain dolls and many other amazing works of art. One of my favourite past times was staring into the cabinets, dreaming of owning one or two of these precious gems beyond the glass. One time, Mrs. Klassen gave me a porcelain doll as a gift. She still sits serenely on my shelf with her porcelain face smiling down at me, her pink knit pants and sweater reminding me of good times in the Klassen house.

Heather was a part of the Klassen family, and although we did a lot of girlie things together, we also did a lot of tomboy things too. On many occasions, we would decide to go out riding motorcycles with the boys. There were a lot more of them than there were of us. But that didn't matter much because Heather owned a red mini-bike that we toured around on. We would fly around a course in their farmyard, with me perched on the small seat behind her.

The course wound its way through granaries and old buildings from days gone by. We made sure we added bumps big enough to give us a real ride. We rode down through the ditches and up the other side. This took real talent and I was glad Heather was at the helm. She was good at knowing what speed to go to make it back up the steep side of the ditch. Sometimes we would even fly down the steep side as fast as we could go. The wind blowing strong in our faces felt so glorious. What wasn't so great was the grasshoppers flying right along with the wind, blasting at your face.

Because we were on a farm, we figured helmets were optional. One time, we came down the hill fine and even conquered the bump up onto the road with ease, but as we sped up for the final race against time, the bike suddenly skidded out from beneath us. We ever so slowly leaned over to one side. For a second I thought maybe we would be able to save the bike from a fall but instead we kept falling until we were more or less under the bike. Heather shut off the bike engine and climbed out from underneath. I was rather stuck. Wearing sandals had not been the best idea of my entire life. My foot was one big bloody mass and I was shocked as it continued to bleed. It had been scraped on the side of the bike as it slid along the dirt road.

Although I would be the last one to admit it I was in quite a bit of pain. Heather found her brother who carried me back to the house. Mrs. Klassen rushed to the door and moved me quickly to the bathroom. She was very careful about getting the temperature of the water perfect. She took hold of my foot and dipped it into the water. It burned like crazy so she took it back out and examined it closely. She discovered small pebbles imbedded in the tender skin on the side of my foot. Finding a pair of tweezers, she pulled out as many of them as she could. I squeezed my eyes shut tightly, trying not to cry out in pain. She patched me up with love and then helped me hobble over to the couch for a rest. I sure got the royal treatment that day, something I knew little about. Of course, when I got home it all ended. I was expected to continue with all the same chores and activities I always had.

ALL REPRIEVE GONE

"And let endurance have its perfect result, that you may be perfect and complete, lacking in nothing."

The Bible

On the outside I was strong but inside I grew weary, tired of the constant struggle for survival, my soul depleted of energy with no way of refilling it. I wished many a time I could restore the fires of life within on my own but this proved too difficult a task for me. Yet another form of denial welled up within me. The only hope of reprieve was to run to a safe place. That meant either the shroud of nature or the comfort of Mrs. Klassen's kind demeanour.

Her house was like a shrine to me. It was almost holy. I would sit on the couch and look at her magical trinkets for hours. There was nothing I wouldn't do for her. I set the table, vacuumed the floor, lovingly dusted her many porcelain creatures. I was a different child at Mrs. Klassen's. Mother would never have recognized me.

Besides, Mrs. Klassen always had gum, usually cinnamon. I would wait patiently for it to come out of its packaging. The sweet, fiery smell made my senses tingle. The first taste was gloriously overwhelming. We never had gum in our house; it was bad for your teeth. Personally, the fact that we were never taken to the dentist was worse for our teeth than the sugar of any gum could ever be, or so I thought. I couldn't continue to live like that, I thought. I had to run away from home.

This is what I dreamed about as I set about making a getaway plan in my mind. I would go out to the garden and pretend to weed the vegetables. Mother would take a quick look out the window and be impressed with my hard-working nature. She would turn away, satisfied that I had learnt my lesson and I would slowly slip away from the garden and onto the path that led to the field behind our house. I would have been remiss if I had not packed a pair of pajamas and my favourite doll in one of Mother's old handbags. This I hid in the bushes around our house to be picked up along the way.

Finally, one day I decided to carry out my plan. In early spring, the field was barren and black. It hadn't rained for awhile so the soil was clumpy and hard. My canvas shoes never fit me properly; they were always hand-me-downs. Often they would slide off as my feet moved awkwardly over the bumpy field. Going directly across the field was at least a half a mile. My feet and back grew weary with the constant struggle to remain upright. By the time I reached the dike road I had to stop. I lay down in the tall grasses of the ditch and rested from my struggles.

I had made it thus far. The rest of the journey would be smooth sailing. I started walking along the dike, drinking in the warmth of the sun and watching the birds fluttering along beside me. The further I walked away, the more content my soul grew. I found safety on that road, alone, my spirit settled in calm serenity. I retrieved a sense of reprieve from deep within. I drank in the freshness of the day, happy with my intended destination. I looked carefully around me. No cars were coming for miles. That was a good sign that Mother had not caught on to my plan, at least not yet.

I almost reached the big road before the lime green, beat-up old half ton drove up beside me. I groaned inwardly. I had been found out. I had one of two choices. Pretend I didn't see the truck or silently get in and admit defeat. The bright day suddenly did not seem so bright. I realized I had no choice but to admit defeat.

Keith picked me up and we drove home in a muted silence. There really was nothing to say. My attempt had been foiled again. Walking out on the road in clear view had been my mistake. I should have gone down the steep ditch through the tall grasses to the other side of the dike so I could remain unseen. My brother's impeccable timing only showed me that my adversary had been watching all the time. She knew just the right time to pick me up and bring me home.

When I first got home, silence ruled. I got the cold, "you've been very bad" treatment. Eventually that wore off, for which I was very sorry. She laid into me on every account. She exploded with anger, shaking uncontrollably. She was livid with my actions. She did not seem to understand my excruciatingly deep longing to never to be a part of her life for as long as I lived. Maybe my dream for freedom was extreme but I had few options as a child. I must deny the reality of Mother's fury and choose a new course of action.

Running away from home only made things worse for me. I remember one incident in which Mother spanked me when I finally tried to sneak back into the house late at night. I had been hiding in the bushes while Andy pedaled past me for hours, never finding me. Mother had sent him. I really didn't care to be found and since Andy had been ordered by Mother to come and collect me he was no longer an ally and as such, could not be trusted.

Most of that day was spent in the peace surrounding me. I picked pieces of the grasses and ripped the heads off, counting the kernels of grain and grass. I swatted a lot of flies and mosquitoes. I found red polka-dotted ladybugs and watched them walk lazily over my skin, then spread their wings and fly away. I wished many times over that I was one of them, flying along on the wind, never caring where it would take me. This was my reprieve. It was my home and I took every chance I could to relish in it. Sure, it brought its consequences but I didn't mind. It wasn't as if Mother yelling at me was anything new. It was a risk I would gladly take.

A NEW CALF

"A newborn child has to cry, for only in this way will his lungs expand. A doctor once told me of a child who could not breathe when it was born. In order to make it breathe the doctor gave it a slight blow. The mother must have thought the doctor cruel. But he was really doing the kindest thing possible. As with newborn children the lungs are contracted, so are our spiritual lungs. But through suffering God strikes us in love. Then our lungs expand and we can breathe and pray."

Sadhu Sundar Singh

The fog lay heavy over the land. You could barely see the little red barn from the farmhouse. The paint was peeling off and the building was rustic and worn. The only reason it was standing was that the cement floor inside stood firm. The smell that emanated from it was strong and forceful, for Father rarely cleaned the manure out of it. He made my older brother, Keith, do it but by the time he got around to it, it was good and caked on. I always felt sorry for the creatures in the barn. The stench was intolerable.

It was Keith's turn to milk the cow that morning but before he even got near the little red barn, he heard a loud, mournful noise coming from it. Alarmed, he raced forward wondering what was going on. As he reached the door and stepped in, he realized our only cow had been in labor all night. He raced back to the house to tell Father but he was nowhere to be found. He ran madly around the yard searching every corner. Father's usual hideout, the shed, was vacant. He called as loudly as he could, hoping for an answer, but only a hollow emptiness answered him back. Father must have taken the half-ton and driven out to the other land to investigate for spring planting. It was no use. He would never find him if this was true. He sighed in frustration.

He ran back to the house to tell Mother. She put her black rubber boots and raincoat on in a hurry. The timing of labor and birth was going to be crucial to Daisy. If not properly cared for, either the cow or the calf might die. She grabbed some pink rubber gloves and made for the barn at a fast pace, Keith right behind her. The path was well worn, which was good, because it was hard to see through the foggy morning. The wailing had not dissipated. The cow was in immense pain.

I heard the ruckus from my bedroom and decided to come and see what the commotion was all about. I slid silently inside to the corner of the barn and watched intently. I felt so sorry for Daisy that I almost started to cry. There was so much confusion. Mother ordered Keith to find clean hay for the birth. He hustled around the small barn and finally decided on a couple of bales from the back corner. Heaving the bale with all his strength, he brought it over and tore it apart. He spread it as evenly as he could around sweet old Daisy and waited for his next order.

By that time Mother was reaching as deep inside the cow as she could with her pretty pink rubber gloves. She let out a loud groan herself; the baby calf was going to be a breech birth and there was no way she could turn that calf around by herself. She knew that was the only way to save the calf but was helpless to do so. She did not have the strength to move the calf without the possibility of breaking a limb. Her nerves got the best of her and she started yelling at Keith to go get Father. Rather than argue that he had already tried, he ran out of the barn in a decided hurry and again started on his futile journey to find Father.

In a split second Mother saw me and ordered me over to the cow. I walked as slowly as I could, trembling all the way. Mother seemed to have control of herself for the moment and tried to be gentle as she told me to stand at the front of the stall and rub Daisy's muzzle to calm her down. I was utterly horrified by just the thought. Shaking in my boots, I crept sideways along the entire length of the stall. Stupefied, I had no idea how I was ever going to accomplish this task. She was a cow, after all, an animal a lot larger than I, scared out her mind and ready to kick anyone or thing that got in her way. I wasn't so sure a nice little rub on the muzzle was all she needed to take the pain away. But now was not the time to argue with Mother. She was totally exasperated with Father for not being there when he should be. She dug in again, doing her best to turn the calf without causing too much damage, but to no avail. It was a hopeless situation. Surely, both Daisy and her baby would perish.

Suddenly, like a thunderbolt, Father barged in through the creaky door, all out of breath. Keith was following obediently behind. As all of this chaos was happening, I stood by Daisy's face rubbing her jaw and praying that something good could come from all of this now that Father was here. Mother was madly tearing off her gloves so she could hand them to Father but before she even got the first one off, Father was on the job.

Diving into the rear of the cow, he forced the calf around and into the proper position for a gory entry into this world. He grabbed the two front legs of the calf and slowly pulled. Daisy bellowed even louder and I rubbed even harder. Father let go as soon as the head appeared. The newborn held what seemed to me to be a sweet expression on its face. But maybe it was not so sweet, for Father did not seem to like the sleepy, contrite look. He opened the calf's mouth and cleared away the slimy, bloody gunk. Daisy heaved one last time and the calf was out, falling into Father's arms. He laid the tired little one down softly on the fresh hay and waited.

We were all counting, waiting for some sign, any sign, of life. The stillness was too quiet, almost frightful; it seemed as if time stopped. Then without warning, we saw what we had all been waiting for. A great, big heave moved the side of the tiny calf. The breaths came faster and faster until we knew without a doubt that she had survived the huge ordeal. I'm not sure, but I think I saw a tear fall down Mother's cheek and for sure, I saw a great sight of relief escape from Father's being.

The newborn calf was rubbed down, freeing her from the unpleasant stickiness of the womb that had kept her warm and cozy for the last months. She looked comforted and happy to be alive as her circulation started to flow. It wasn't long before she struggled to her feet, wobbling hither and thither. I weaved and bobbed with her, holding my hands out to catch her in case she fell. Father continued the rubbing and he was quite vigorous about it. Holding her on both sides, he used long strokes to make her coat shiny. Mama cow was standing patiently, knowing what was coming next. She looked tuckered out from all her trials and like she could sleep for a thousand years. The calf bawled insistently and took her first few steps over to her Mother. She started suckling eagerly on her Mother's teat, hungry over her arduous entry into this world. Daisy was very patient with her newborn and warmed to her immediately, licking her coat with her rough tongue.

Clean-up consisted of getting rid of the birthing hay and putting down fresh straw. We were all filthy with a mixture of manure and slop from the cow and calf. That did not mean our job was done. Shovels and pitchforks were raised and the straw flew furiously into the wheelbarrow to be burnt ever so sanitarily. Father decided he was exhausted so headed back to the house for a good cleaning.

The old heater in one corner of the smelly old barn was turned on for a little extra warmth on this cold spring morning. Daisy was given clean water and extra oats to eat which she gobbled down gratefully. It really was quite the scene. All of us sat back and watched the miracle that had just occurred. We were a sight for sore eyes, weary and shaken by the near-death experience of the soft-eyed calf, the newest family member.

A watchful eye was kept on the baby for the next twenty-four hours solid. Keith was assigned to this task. I never really knew how he felt about it but I figured it couldn't be that hard watching over the Mother/daughter pair. Every time I took a peek in the barn, there seemed to be a warm glow coming from them. They stood close to one another, licking and bawling, forming a close bond. I was almost jealous of their closeness; it surely was nothing I had ever felt with my parents.

IN SICKNESS

I came home from school only to find Mother was in the hospital. To seek out any information whatsoever from Father was like pulling teeth. He lived in his own little world of paranoia and fear. I knew that Mother was suffering from breast cancer. I surmised that she had had a mammogram and that's how the dreaded disease was discovered.

Back then, little could be done but to cut out the offending disease. It was the seventies after all. Her sudden surgery left her in excruciating pain. Her one shoulder was all but useless, yet she never complained.

Children were not allowed in the hospital room in those days, so Father went all alone. He was gone for hours at a time, never really telling anyone of us when he would be home. His disappearance meant that we children were left to fend for ourselves, which was never a good thing. Joy ordered us all around, taking over the Mother role. Keith and I battled for control and I rebelled against any authority he thought was his. Little brother chose indifference. He was obviously the smartest of us all. He watched TV, played with the dog, shot his .22 rifle, did anything but involve himself in the tiny conquests that were won and lost.

Interjected in between these domestic wars were TV dinners and ice cream. Father was so exhausted from his visits with Mother that he brought home a new kind of processed dinner each night. For him, the least amount of work possible was the only choice.

As children, we thought this was great. We forgot our squabbling for the day and dove into the scrumptious boxed meals. Ever new and different, they provided a welcome relief from the major frustration of the day.

Father looked ever weary. The deep furrow in his brow became very pronounced with time. He leaned against the table and rubbed his forehead as though in the rubbing, the worry would all go away. He spoke little. He showed no emotion. He assumed we all knew our duties and would do them without being told, and so we did. Of course, cleaning up after TV dinners did not really involve too much. Washing glasses and cutlery was no big hardship.

I did my best not to stir the waters when Father was around. I helped obediently, wondering if any information about Mother would be forthcoming, but there never was anything much. While we worked the best we could to create a sense of normalcy in the home, Father sat in his favourite chair. It was a tattered blue easy chair set by the fake fireplace in the living room. He pushed it back as far as it would go and just lay there with his eyes closed tight, not moving, his face all scrunched up. It wouldn't really have mattered what we did. He just lay there like he was dying, holding his chest with his arms crossed one over the other. And maybe he was dying; after all, there was no one to fight with anymore. His world had completely changed.

Not one of us had the gumption to ask him questions about Mother's health. We knew we could not move him to be involved with us in any way. We just left him be. We watched a lot of television, anything to distract ourselves from a situation we did not know how to handle. It was more than obvious to us who the communicator in the family was now that Mother was gone. Our lame attempts to comfort each other were small and pitiful. A pat on the shoulder, a tousle of the hair, there really wasn't much more to do.

Our escape from all of this aloneness was school. We were always at the bus on time, no exceptions. I don't think any of us really wanted to come home. There was no home to come to. It was a time of darkness and confusion. Our bodily need for food was taken care of but that was about it. The emotional and personal connection to a warm body was sadly and desperately missing.

The void went on until the day Mother finally came home. That was the only clue we had that she must have made it through her awful ordeal. She had come out on the other side and home to us.

It was unfortunate that we remained solitary while Mother was in the hospital but on the other hand it gave me a lot of time to think things through, mainly my relationship with Mother. In some very odd way I knew she loved me. She always did her best to save us from Father's unfriendly advances. On occasion, she would buy us a little something when she went shopping. She even tried to make each of us our favourite supper from time to time.

But as for warmth, there was very little. Most of the time, I separated myself from her to the point where she was no longer my Mother. She was a person I lived with. But facing the fact that she may die had me grasping at straws. Surely, there was a way to let her into my heart. The few kindnesses she offered me from time to time were the only things I had to take hold of. It was a small warmth inside me with an ever deeper hollowness in behind. There really was no use trying to create relationship now. It was too late.

Father's remedy for recuperation was to whisk Mother off to Hawaii. She complained more about having to go than about her experience with cancer. She was in a great amount of pain from the surgery. They had taken the skin from her shoulder and used it to create a sort of new skin over the cavity that had been her breast. She had an extremely difficult time moving her shoulder around in a circular motion. She suffered in silence, not wanting anyone to know the true extent of her journey through the cancer. She never shared her personal journey with the life-shattering disease with anyone; it was either much too difficult for her to say, or better left unsaid.

After the vacation with Father was when she really began to move ahead in her recovery. Her green, velour housecoat was stamped on her. It had worn in all the right places. I am sure she wore it because of her shoulder. Everything else was too tight around her wounded shoulder from surgery.

She spent a lot of time in her favourite chair reading. She dozed off and on and did only the basics of housework. Luckily, it was winter so the dreaded growing, waiting, and harvest season was not yet upon us. This new Mother was kind and good. She listened and spoke in turn. There was little room for admonishment. I almost wanted to spend time with her.

The doctor had given her some exercises to loosen up her shoulder. The pain was excruciating, but that never deterred her from pushing ahead. Her stamina was at its best.

CHARGED

By the time I reached the house from where the big yellow school bus had dropped me off, it was time for a little afternoon snack. Everything was left in an impossible mess. The boys had already created their sandwiches piled high with peanut butter, likely more of it than the bread itself. Peanut butter covered the table, the jar of apricot jam lying ever so close to toppling off the table. A loaf of bread chucked to the side onto the counter, half finished.

I went to work grabbing this and that; I really was no better than my brothers. I savoured the peanut butter and jam as it slid down my throat. I could see the orioles and finches from my perch on my kitchen chair. Mother faithfully fed the birds and in return they praised her with their glorious song and vibrant colours of yellow and orange.

My sister came down the stairs only to mumble something about all the chores that needed to be done before Mother got home from work. I did my best to ignore this intrusion on my happy little world but her insistent voice did not recede. The grating sound of her voice continued as I went on eating my sandwich. I was never sure why it was me she chose to torment when two non-innocent brothers lay on their respective couches in the living room picking their noses.

I was to tidy the dining room and the living room before Mother got home. I nodded my head, pretending I understood and would surely complete the tasks, but her nagging voice droned on. My next ploy was to get up and go into the dining room as if I would go about the ordered tasks. Instead I sat down on the dining room table as close as I could get to the television and began watching my favourite afternoon drivel. My location was no tactical error. From here I could see Mother driving up the road and with the touch of a button, the TV could be off and I could be tidying up like the good little girl I was.

Overtones of a coup could be heard rising up from the other room. Joy was creating a counter-attack for my general lack of performance. I reached out to shut down the TV, but as I moved my arm up towards the set a hand grabbed my arm, and I pulled away. As familiar as I was with this method to bring me under control, this attack formed from a long standing coalition between older brother and sister, shocked me again and again.

As the war began I wrenched my arm away and fled in the opposite direction. Hiding under the table gave me a few moments of freedom. I kicked every which way to prevent the inevitable. Gathering my bearings I devised a plan and shot out from under the table. I was in open space now and had to be quick about my plan. Adrenaline pumping, I burst forth and made a lunge for the dark hallway that led to the safety of a bathroom and a lockable door.

At times my plan worked, at times it failed. Today it failed. A monstrous foot sent me flying over onto my back into a brown paneled wall. By now, a knowingly weaker person would have given into this distinctive pattern of power, but not I. I was fast, and I drew upon that strength. I dipped and dived over and around his hulking body, but in the end he had me right where he wanted me, at the edge of the basement stairs. I gathered the last bit of strength I had and lunged through his gangly legs. I was trapped. He pushed me slowly at first, laughing a sinister laugh, down into the deep, dark dungeon, then kicked hard, not caring where his foot hit. My body was sore all over but still my will was my own.

I was sopping wet with sweat from the constant struggle for freedom. Welts were forming on my arms and legs. My quick darts and dashes had proven no match for these army-like tactics. I was dragged to one of the usual spots--the basement telepost that stood strong and steady in spite of my struggles.

The brilliant orange skipping rope performed its secret ritual, binding me to itself. Cold seeped into body and enveloped my soul. Tired from my arduous struggle, I slumped down and grew very still. I watched the bugs crawling along the basement floor. It had always been a wet, dark place, prone to breeding all the exotics like earwigs, big black beetles, even spiders weaving their webs in mysterious places.

Reluctantly I became very still. The fight was over. I forced myself to become very still. Closing my eyes, I tried to imagine something new and shiny; usually this had no effect on the pain from the tight ropes wound around my wrist and ankles.

While he savoured each movement he made of inflicting more pain, I cried out silently in my mind for redemption. I did not even know what it was I really wanted except, at the very least, to be released from this nightmare. I pondered what I had done to deserve this torture. My mind tried desperately to cling to some sense of sanity, but I found none. The only freedom was denial and that is what I chose, strong and unwavering. I began to dream, to soar above the clouds into a magic kingdom made only for me, a kingdom where I was touched by good and good alone. In the real world, I was left tied up to the pole in the basement, bound in darkness, rejected by my small world.

A secret code spoken released me at the exact moment Mother came home. The release from the orange skipping rope was a welcome relief from the torture that had racked my body from the time I had raced home from school to the second before one of my parents drove on the yard. But the constant reminder of the torture to come was never far from my mind. I had to be on constant alert.

SKUNKED

Looking out the window was one of our favoured past times. The bantam hen and her half-grown chicks were rooting and turning up the grass trying to find grubs for a late but speedy breakfast. The colouring on their feathers shone in the sunlight. Spots of browns and reds gleaned in the sun as they grew in the safety of our yard.

Joy had a small dog named Ginger. She was brown and black. For some reason, Mother showed favouritism towards her, for she was the only dog that ever got to stay indoors. She did a few tricks and got fed many scraps from the table, mostly by Andy. He was a little fussy about what he ate so he gave treats to Ginger on the sly, or so he thought. If the dog wouldn't take them he would feign going to the bathroom and promptly deposit them behind the old piano in the living room. Mother had refinished it and it was stunning. Inside the soundboard was cracked making it difficult to play.

Although Ginger, my sister's dog, was never fixed, she also never had puppies. That is, until she was very old. I think she was around ten or eleven in people years when she decided to create life in her belly. I begged and begged to keep one of the puppies. I was most excited of all when Mother said I could, a promise I am sure that came out of her own weakness for dogs.

The poor old girl suffered through labour and delivery and out came five healthy pups. They were all different colours but the one that caught my eye was a sandy brown and very fluffy. I spent all my days in the garage watching over the litter, chattering away to them as if they could understand me. I am almost sure that the fluffy one would practically look me in the eye as I went on and on about absolutely nothing. The new Mother and crew were in a wooden crate at the very back of the big red garage. It was a cozy little hole that kept the pups warm, dry, and well fed by their new old Mother.

Setting the last pup down one day, I looked at them all together in their safe home. They were adorable but I was getting hungry myself just watching them eat and needed to go into the house for some lunch. It was noon and my stomach was grumbling. I washed my hands and sat down to lunch. It was just Mother, Andy, and me today so it could actually prove to be a pleasant time.

Father was off to the other land, almost five miles away, to check on his fields. He would just stand in there amongst the budding wheat, watching the wind blow the stalks back and forth. Sometimes he would bend down, tearing off a head and crumbling it in his hands, he would count the kernels that fell lazily onto to his palm. He would consider the bumper crop that would come in the fall. He was more than satisfied in his ability as a farmer. He was feeding a hungry world, as ungrateful and unaware as they were. His mission was complete. His obsession with his grain farming left us relaxed and peaceful for the time being.

We prayed and dove into our food. It was pretty much the same every day. Ham sausage, cheese and tomatoes with tons of mayo and mustard, and let's not forget Mother's homemade bread. It tasted so good, I savoured every moment of it melting in my mouth as chewed slowly. Oh, and it smelled good too filling up the whole house with its delicious presence.

As we ate in silence all three of us stared out the window at the wondrous day. There was so much to see. The sky was blue, the sun shining brightly. There were the proud cats with their litters of kittens wobbling behind them. Squirrels were chasing each other, dashing up and down tree branches, madly trying to prove their agility. There were sparrows, gold finches, starlings, and woodpeckers - far too many kinds of birds to count. The big goose stood guarding the pond in the background. I knew enough not to get in his way. He could have his territory; I had been honked at and bitten one too many times. The bantam hens and her chicks were strutting around the yard, occasionally pecking at some unsuspecting prey in the grass or gravel. The trees and bushes swayed ever so slightly in the breeze.

Mother chattered on and on about everything she had to do, and believe me it was an extensive list. The major task of the day was to get the vegetable garden into shape. That meant a lot of mindless weeding and watering too. The garden grew extra thirsty during July and August. There was less rain and more blue sky, causing everything to grow at a fast pace.

I was half listening while Andy wolfed down his third piece of homemade bread with peanut butter and honey. The pleasure on his face told the tale. But slowly his satisfaction grew to consternation. He pointed out the window, his final mouthful going down to its destiny. Then he shook his hand and tried to get out a muffled version of a sentence. Both Mother and I looked out the window but saw nothing. He took a final swallow and pointed again, this time with more passion. This time we could understand his words. "There's a skunk going into the garage."

We almost laughed; after all, skunks were nocturnal creatures. They were no more capable of wandering around in the daylight than a fish could swim on land. But the animal caught my Mother's eye too. She stared and realized it was dragging itself by its front legs; its rear end was useless.

She jumped up and said, "The puppies." She feared for the safety of the tiny animals. She was out the door before we were even up off our chairs. It was obvious the situation was dire. We raced after her to the garage. By this time, the squealing was horrendous. The puppies were fighting for their lives and Mama Ginger was defending their very existence. She was growling and barking, but it seemed the skunk was gaining the upper hand. Each yelp paralyzed me further, my brother too.

Mother yelled some sense into us. At her command, we jumped up onto the car for safety. We all shouted and screamed for the skunk to get away from the cherished dogs but he stubbornly sunk his teeth into their baby skin, causing blood to flow. Watching the scenario, I began to cry. How could this be happening?

Mother yelled out another command, "Go get the .22 rifle." Andy readily complied; he didn't want to listen to the helpless cries any longer. He came back shaking like a leaf. The skunk, having done his dirty deed, was slowly pulling himself out of the garage. Andy hoisted the rifle into the air, aimed and fired. The car now officially had a ding in it. His hands were shaking so hard he could not aim with any efficiency. I jumped down off the car and ran towards him. I steadied the barrel of the gun with my hands, aiming it at this mean-spirited thing. Andy caught on right away and shot the gun again. It took three shots to finally kill the thing and when it was all over, we sank to our knees. We looked at each other in grim satisfaction. We had brought in our first kill and punctured the garden tractor tired in the process.

After a few moments, we gathered ourselves together and went to look at the damage. Mother warned us not to touch the puppies. Ginger lay on her side, heaving her last breath. She had defended her litter, sacrificing herself for them. The scene was awful.

Mother headed for the house to call the Ministry of Natural Resources. She said we had to find out if the skunk was rabid. After staring at the mangy skunk for a while, watching for any signs of life, we left the scene and returned to the crying puppies. It was more than tempting to pick them up and comfort them, but Mother had said not to touch them. She said this in her most serious voice and so we complied. It wasn't long before she came running back, saying the MNR guy would be here shortly. Whatever she said on the phone must have been serious for him to come so quickly. You could tell she felt helpless. She just stood there wringing her hands. This was a state we did not see our Mother in too often. She usually knew exactly what to do

By now, I was crying silently, wanting to pick up my sandy brown fluffy puppy and cradle him in my arms. He looked so forlorn just lying there, trying to lick the skunk's saliva off of himself.

I don't know how long we all stood there assessing the situation before we heard a truck come on the yard. Sure enough, it was the MNR man. He talked to Mother for a long time and then went right to work. I think it was a Saturday so he said he would have the results to us by the beginning of next week.

In the meantime, we were to quarantine all of our animals, for the sake of safety. He had cages of all kinds with him and told us to lock up the dogs and the cats. I thought he must have been joking; either that or he had never tried to catch a half-wild cat and put it behind bars. We all set to work at this impossible task while he chopped off the skunk's head. Apparently that's all he needed to make a correct diagnosis.

Pretty well everything was taken care of by the time Father came wheeling onto the yard. Mother and he had a deep and serious talk about what to do next. I knew they were deciding on which animals lived and which ones died. That night, Father took a black garbage bag for the pups and his rifle for Ginger and did the hideous task of consigning the dogs to a special doggie heaven somewhere beyond this world.

I dared not ask about my fluffy puppy but when I went and searched in the garage, there was Sandy, as I had so aptly named him. They had saved him for me. This was one of the few acts of kindness I ever received from my parents. It brought a broad smile to my face as I gently talked to my dog. He had been saved for me after all.

Mother was very serious when I came back from visiting with Sandy. She said I was not allowed to touch him for six to eight weeks. I could walk him and take care of him, but I could not allow him to lick me. She did not want me getting rabies too. My resolve, and I suppose Mothers too, lasted about a week or two. Then I began petting him and holding him. I didn't really realize how serious the situation was. It wasn't too much later that Mother caught me at it. The next morning when I went to feed Sandy he was gone. I called and called, he didn't come. The realization sunk in. My Sandy was now in heaven too.

"I postpone death by living, by suffering, by error, by risking, by giving, by losing."

Anaïs Nin

HEAVEN CAME DOWN

One day, I decided that I wanted to discover more about God. I was eleven, too young, some said, to be baptized into the fold. However, I really wanted to be accepted by at least someone. It was hard enough to tell Mother about wanting to be baptized but she said if I were at all serious about it, I had to go to the pastor and talk to him.

Now I was just a little bit afraid of the pastor. He was an older gentleman with white, white hair. I think he wore a toupee, which always made me chuckle, only to myself of course. On Sundays, he would stand at the front door of the church and shake hands as people went in. It wasn't as if he was really our pastor because he only came out on Sundays to preach. It sounds a bit strange but I guess our little church didn't have enough money for a full-time pastor.

When he stood at the front of the church, he would say, "Our passage this morning is taken from…" Then a member of the congregation would get up and read it. Sometimes it was even my Father. My Father had these long sideburns with his hair parted on the side. His hair kept falling down to hide his eyes and he had to swipe it away. I guess he was blessed with a full head of hair. He read intently and with great authority as though he owned the words. This seemed strange to me and I could not understand how this Sunday morning man and the one I saw on a daily basis could coexist. I hate to use the word "hypocrite" for my own Father, but that was what I had come to believe about him. He was one person in front of the church congregation and a totally different person in secret. What other word could be used?

A couple of times, if I looked intently at the pastor behind the pulpit, he had an odd glowing light behind him. I always thought it was the spirit of God shining down on him. I figured if he was a pastor he must be pretty close to God so the bright light made a lot of sense to me. I greatly admired him because of the glow, wondering when he would get taken up to heaven because he was so good. I couldn't help thinking he must have been as good as Enoch from the Bible, who got carried up to heaven and never had to die. Some days I sure wished I would be carried up like that.

I would stare at him as he spoke, never really even hearing a word that came out of his mouth. I think he must have been a pretty dull speaker because a lot of people in the back rows would sit with folded arms, their heads lolling back and forth. I think some of them even drooled out of the corner of their mouths. I'm not sure why they came to church. Maybe they couldn't get a good rest at home.

When the service was over, they would greet the pastor at the door and tell him what a good message he had. They would pull a profound phrase from their repertoire and breathe a sigh of relief when the pastor said thank you.

So this was the person I had to talk to about being baptized. I was apparently the youngest person ever in the church to ask to be baptized. His response to me was fantastic. He said he was very happy for me. Taking this step of faith would be an important part of my walk with Christ. I can't say that I knew what a step of faith was, but I didn't really care because this seemed to correlate with a resounding yes! I could be baptized into God's family.

As he talked to me more I realized that I would have to share my testimony in front of the whole church membership and then be subjected to various questions from that same membership. My face fell; this sounded like a lot of work, since speaking in public had never been my thing. I had thought that baptism was a personal thing between Jesus and me, not a circus act where you were walking on a tightrope or jumping through hoops. All I had wanted was to be closer to Jesus.

I struggled through writing my testimony, trying to make life sound a little more glamorous than it actually was. I left out certain aspects and tried to dwell on the good. I don't think I even got a full page of stuff before my Mother took over, commenting on all the glorious experiences in my life. She created a life of which I knew nothing about. Family devotions were ever-so-wholesome; family suppers created care and support for another day; working together provided a challenge and courage to do better.

Although I knew nothing of this "Brady Bunch" family, this is what everyone in the church heard the day of my testimony. The hope that I presented to the congregation of a life filled with prosperity and joy was a mere illusion to me. But nothing mattered so long as I could be baptized and find this new life in Christ I was dreaming about.

Most of the people accepted my small rendition of my life with unwavering faith, all nodding their heads in my favour. However, one man relentlessly barraged me with questions. I felt like logs of a fire being poked by a stick. The fire was slowly and painfully going out only to be stabbed again. I am sure I looked like a wild cat cornered by an angry Doberman. I did not know whether to put my hackles up or surrender to the onslaught of questioning. I was in unfamiliar territory but suddenly something I said must have satisfied this parishioner for the onslaught came to an end. I became calm and relaxed. Something I said had appeased the old codger. I was free to become baptized.

The day finally arrived. We drove into the large metropolis of Winnipeg. Reaching the church did not take long. As we entered the doors, it struck me. There was no turning back. I was doing this for good.

Four or five others were being baptized at the same time. We all went back stage and put on white gowns. The Mennonites believe in full immersion. I was scared I might never come up again but I did my best to trust the pastor to pull me back out of the water. The tank was at the back of the stage. I can't remember where I was in line but it felt like an incredibly long time before it was my turn. I shook as I walked down the stairs into the water. The gown floated to the surface and I had to hold it down with my hands. This was a slightly awkward moment as I looked like I was in a straightjacket.

My pastor was waiting for me, kindly holding out his hand for me to come to him. He whispered, "Peace, be still" in my ear. He talked for a while but I didn't hear a thing--I was too nervous about being dunked. He grabbed both my hands in his--they were crossed together on my chest--held my back and gently forced me down under the water. The words, "I baptize you in the name of the Father, the Son and the Holy Ghost," were on the lips of my pastor. I gulped in a big chunk of air and held my breath.

Then I was under and up before I knew it. The rapture I felt was beyond words. It was as if I had ascended into heaven itself. There was complete and glorious peace. The sweetness of the moment was known only to Jesus and me. I was assured of God's love in my life and that it would last forever. Nothing could take away the stillness, the fulfillment of that day. Jesus descended on me like a dove. Now I realize that all that sounds like a whole bunch of religious jargon, but my longing for someone to love me was very strong. Jesus was my last chance and He came through that day in an amazing way.

MOODY, MOODY MOTHER

"Suffering has been stronger than all other teaching, and has taught me to understand what your heart used to be, I have been bent and broken, but – I hope – into a better shape."

Charles Dickens

It was often too hard to hold onto the peace I'd felt on the day of my baptism.

On days like today, Mother was ruthless. She got into ruts and never seemed to get out. It was Saturday chore day and no matter which task I performed it was like a cherished recipe gone wrong. Although the disappointment over a bad recipe may subside quickly, Mother's disappointment in me grew steadily. Today, I was spanked repeatedly with the black leather belt.

Tattered and torn, it was held on a special hook in the kitchen cabinet. That leather belt came down hard on my young skin. I had not completed a job well enough. I was constantly lazing my day away. I spent too much time daydreaming and not enough doing the menial tasks Mother chose to push on me. She didn't seem to realize that this form of punishment, the abhorrent spanking, only created a hardness in what was once a soft heart.

I had to bend over the white metal garbage can, with rusted edges, in the small kitchen. I was then subjected to the complete humiliation of being spanked all the way up to the age of sixteen. My gangly body did its best to comply but it was no easy task. I was tall and lanky. Crumpling down to the low level of the garbage can created a bend in me, folding me like an accordion. The slashing across my rear end didn't even hurt anymore and for this I was proud. The whip used to spank my bruised backside slid down my legs and up my back, a symbol of the unending abuse I had grown to understand as a part of my young life. I was never separate from it.

Suffering followed me around life like an obedient puppy, never far away. There were times when Mother tried so hard to get me to respond appropriately to her method of corporal punishment that I honestly believe it hurt her more than me. She would become bright red in the face, her eyes full of fury. She became extremely frustrated in her demeanour, often unable to control her caustic tone. I would smile to myself inside, knowing that I had won the war for control. She was helpless to rule over me.

In times like these, when my attempts to go against the accepted family system wore on her beyond her ability to control her deep-seated anger, she would often call for Father. He would leave his work behind with a heavy sigh. He would walk slowly to the house, knowing his duty would leave him worn. His methods were even more gruesome than Mother's were. His aim to my backside was perfect. He never missed in his timing. One…two…three…all the way to ten. He would drive the belt deep into my skin, the purple welts swollen in direct proportion to his ability to consistently plant the belt in the same spot.

Unlike Mother, the whole ordeal seemed to make him sad. It was an onerous task to him. It was as if he despised the pain Mother pushed him to inflict on me. He eyes reached out with compassion but his hand remained heavy. His knew the drill, he knew his part, and he knew the outcome. Nothing, nothing would come of it. Life would go on the same as before. Mother would be unable to control her anger against me and I would rebel against her authority.

RAMBLING ON

One day, I was all alone in my room. It was somewhere I needed to be. I went there every day after school in hopes of a little reprieve. My bed was by the window so I would sit totally still on my comfortable blankets and look outside. It was a part my daily routine.

I opened the sticky window frame, painted over one too many times, to feel the breeze. Sometimes it was soft and sometimes it blew hard, but its freshness always flowed into the room. I saw the tall pine tree just outside my window. Its needles were many shades of green, and if you thought long and hard enough you could actually feel its prickly points on your skin. I always looked for the purple and yellow pansies in Mother's garden below. They came up brand new every year. They were so delicate-looking. I heard the tiny birds singing their songs--swallows, sparrows, chickadees. The sky was extra blue that day. I breathed a sigh of relief. Nature had a calming effect on me. It was a release from the pressures of the day, a way to get away from the chaos of my family.

Mother would sit at the kitchen table, waiting for us to come home. She would smile hopefully at me, wondering every day if I would sit down for a chat after school, but I mostly just ran up the stairs as quickly as I could. I didn't want to take the chance of stopping and having to listen to Mother's exceptionally boring day. The way she talked about Father was nothing but derogatory. Neighbours and friends were no different. Mrs. Klassen spent too much time shopping and not enough cleaning. Mrs. Koop was a gossip and to be avoided at all time. Even her best friend, Mrs. Sawatsky, had gained too much weight in the later days and needed to go on a special diet. I really do not remember hearing anything good about anybody or any part of her day. So I had one of two choices. I would stare out the window, occasionally nodding my head at her comments, or I would resort to the much-relished option of running up the stairs and letting my sister have the privileged position across from my Mother. I felt a little sorry for Joy but not sorry enough to put myself in the position of a Mother to a daughter. I remained undaunted and grew even more reclusive. I wanted nothing more than to be as far away from Mother as possible.

BIG RED

It was that time of year again. The sweet smell of fall filled the air. Father, on the other hand, smelled of sweat and grease whenever he came in the door. Sometimes he remembered to take off his filthy rubber boots when he came in, but it was a gamble every time to see if he would or wouldn't. We kids made bets, but having no money, it didn't really matter what happened. He was usually in quite a state, frantic with worry.

Keith was always the first to be yelled at by him. He was comfortable, sitting on Fathers' reclining chair absorbed in one book or another. His long, gangly legs went into gear when he heard the door open. Pushing the chair into the upright position he jumped up and leapt across the living room floor. I am sure I saw sparks flying out from behind him on one or two occasions. Father had his orders for his oldest son. He was to refill the combine with gas, readying it for its next trip to the field. Keith flew past Father, not wanting to feel the slap of his hand on the back of his head.

There was no point in arguing with this man. He was at the top of the food chain, everything being eaten around him, his mouth open wide. As long as we kept moving quickly, not bothering to turn around and have a look at what was chasing us, we would survive. This environment of authoritarianism was all I knew as a child.

Father looked around for someone else to pick on. His eyes met with Mother's. They quietly reminded him it was Saturday morning, chore time. He did not challenge these eyes. Instead he dashed for the door, following Keith outside. This did not bode well for Keith. He had no escape and would have to listen to Father's constant put-downs as he slaved for his very life. We girls were left to fend for ourselves against Mother. Each chore had to be executed to perfection. There was no allowance for an extra smudge on the window or a crumb left on the counter. It felt like we were in the army shining our shoes over and over until we got the task correct. Although I did not relish Keith's position in the family, I wasn't too fond of my own either. I had a choice between being either stupid, wrong and just a plain idiot for most of my growing up life. None of those options particularly appealed to me as there was no subtlety to them. They were spoken out loud and with force.

I was sitting quietly by myself reading a novel. The couch was old and coloured with bright red flowers. It was full of pulls and pills so I sat curled up in a blanket. The couch fabric was extremely worn in spots and downright dirty in others. It was also as hard as a brick. This was the best piece of furniture we had in the house in those days.

The couch's foibles didn't really matter much to me anyway because I was completely lost in my book. Nobody could shake me away from it. I always had a book in my face, yet another chosen way of escape. However, this time the voice I heard was growing louder and louder so I decided to look up on the off chance that someone was actually talking to me. There stood Father, right up in my face, barking out some order or other. I tried smiling sweetly but he only got louder. Apparently, it was raining outside, nothing that his dear weather radio had told him about.

Keith and Joy had already been told to close up the top of the metal bins. This was a dangerous task, climbing a wobbly ladder to the bin roof and then climbing another ladder even higher up the roof to the top. The lid was dropped over the hole to the bin and then latched tight. This is where things got dicey. With the rain and the wind driving in their faces, my siblings never felt very secure at the top. Although they never plunged to their deaths, this was an arduous task they came to hate.

I, on the other hand, was to go outside, dash to the big red farm truck and drive it into the shed. It held a special cargo of grain in it that could not get wet. Not only had Father left it out in the field, but there was no tarp over it in case of such emergencies. My eyes might as well have rolled right out of my head. At the ripe age of ten I had never driven the truck before. What was Father thinking? But there was no time for such questions, only for obedience. I dragged my rubber boots out and put them on, added my raincoat and ran across the yard and into the field. Sure enough, the big red truck was waiting for me on the other side of the bushes. Stumbling across the freshly harvested field, I climbed up into the driver's seat. It smelled earthy in the cabin, a scent I had grown to love.

No explanation had been given on how to start, shift or drive this big monstrosity so I just made things up as I went along. I knew you had to push the clutch in so I did that and tried the key, a perfect start. Now I had no clue what should come next. Letting out the clutch seemed right so I did that and the truck came to a sudden halt. I was missing a step somewhere. I knew where the gas and the brake were, it must have something to do with them.

I started the truck again and this time I pushed on the gas as I let out the clutch. It lunged forward only to stall again a little ways down the field. I cannot say I ever mastered that truck. We pretty much did the same dance again and again down the field until we got onto the yard. It had no power steering, and as far as I was concerned the opening to the shed looked awfully narrow. Somehow I made it through without crashing into anything. Relief was my best reaction. I never wondered at a Father who would force me to do something and give me no direction on how to do it. That was just a part of life.

I may have learnt more about how to stall a vehicle than about driving one that day, but my true driving lessons came later in life from Keith. The old, lime green half ton was perfect for my lessons. With Keith in the passenger's seat, I climbed in and settled myself properly in the drivers' seat of the smelly truck. Lifting the seat lever up, I tried to position my feet perfectly for some solid clutch/brake/gas pedal action.

Keith had already positioned us in the middle of the yard so I could do no damage to other vehicles and possibly even buildings. He had the patience of Job. Most of my first lesson consisted of stalling, stalling and then stalling. Good thing she was a good-tempered old truck or she might have bucked me off.

As the lessons progressed, we made our way slowly down the driveway. I wasn't too sure I wanted to reach the end because then I would have to turn the steering wheel as well as press on the gas. With no power steering on this cheap old Ford I would have to force the wheel with all my might to get her going. But turn onto the road we did.

We made it all the way to four corners, which was a quarter of a mile down the road. Then Keith wanted me to turn around. What happened next created a few little snickers from my brother. The harder I cranked and turned that wheel, the more I accelerated and braked, the more I pushed the gearshift into first and reverse, the deeper I got into the ditch. It didn't seem to matter what I did, that old truck was pulled like a magnet into a vast chasm with a puddle of water deep down below.

We were facing straight down into the ditch on a steep slant when Keith finally pulled the emergency brake, opened his door and got out. Without a word, he walked around the leaning truck. I moved over with relief and watched as he manhandled the truck out of the ditch and up onto the gravel road. When the wheels were straight on with the gravel ruts in the road, I took over again. Once again, I conked out the engine, jerking the truck to many a halt. Still no word from my brother; his silence was unnerving. But I have to say I rather enjoyed those driving lessons. They were one of the few times Keith and I got along.

ASSEMBLY OF THE CHICKENS

Fall came with the same clear precision as it always did. The leaves grew colourful and bright. The fields were barren after the harvest. The end of the season meant a little less busyness and lot more relaxation, but not before slaughtering day.

We had all helped the whole summer long to keep the chickens in the chicken coop where they belonged. At first they were fuzzy and cute. You could sit down in the pen with them and pet them, catching them one by one. Gradually they grew larger. They looked funny with a few feathers and lots of fuzz, but they were still oh so much fun to play with.

I made sure they had water. A bit of reddish purple medicine went into each jar. It was great fun to turn the water jars over and watch the water burble out to a certain point and then stop.

The poor chickens had to eat the same pellet food day after day. Once I even tried a piece to see what it was like. I can't say it was particularly tasty.

The more the little munchkins grew, the worse the stink in the coop got. After awhile, no one could stand it anymore. I ran in, holding my nose, quickly executing my duties (I talked away to them as though they were long lost friends), and then made a quick retreat.

As the summer passed, Mother and I constructed a fence around the old porch coop. This way the chickens could get a little fresh air. The small white feathered creatures loved it outside. They would all rush to get through the porch door every morning. They were getting so big they filled up the entire outside yard. They jumped and squawked around and over each other, creating havoc in their newfound space.

There were several foxes that tried their hardest to grab a fancy chicken dinner to take home with them. Andy and I got the job of finding extra boards to close up the holes at the bottom and sides of the coop. I must say for all the times I banged my fingers with the hammer I still loved nailing those boards onto the old porch. I was protecting a living creature from becoming a fox's dinner, and chicken, after all, was my favourite dish.

One red, lean fox did not give up on his hunt. He came around at night when we were all snuggled in our beds and seized a chicken or two. So every morning we renewed our efforts to create safety for the flock. In fact, one year we even put an electric fence all the way around the coop to scare the carnivore off. We hoped to bring ourselves some peace of mind from this sleek predator's assaults. But he outsmarted us and one year got five of the juicy beauties.

Although I blame the fox for most of the deaths, the stealthy badger did his share of damage too. The fox was quick about the kill, but the badger took his time, digging under the fence and waiting for the opportune moment to strike. He shook his prey back and forth in his mouth, mauling it to death. I much preferred the fox's method.

Now that fall was here, slaughtering day came with it. There were several different stations to prepare. The chopping block was planted firmly on the solid ground in the coop. It was the same old piece of wood stained with a reminder of the year before.

My Father sharpened the axe until it glinted in the sunlight. You could slice your finger easily in one quick motion. Then there were the huge nails driven into the two by fours on the top of the porch rafters and a couple of pails of scalding hot water to go beside the nails.

Last, but not least, was the eviscerating table, an old picnic table covered with a plastic tablecloth. This cloth was disinfected to within an inch of its life. The three centers were where the chickens we had nurtured all summer long would meet their end. The defenseless critters were going to become a sad statistic and a gourmet meal for us all at once. Slaughtering day!

Joy definitely had the more delightful job of the two of us. She was to hold each chicken's neck down tight while Mother held the chicken's body still. Then before you knew it, the sound of the axe created havoc in the chicken pen as it flew through the air, through the chicken's neck and into the chopping block. Blood splattered itself everywhere, the outside of the porch, the still living flock and even Mother and Joy's clothes and faces. It was a gruesome act. What came next was the biggest laugh of all. Mother laid down a pile of hay beside the coop and we watched and giggled at the chicken (with no head) running around on the straw every which way. Mother explained scientifically that the chickens muscles where still moving even in their demise. After a few minutes, it flopped over to its final death and then it was my turn to take over.

Mother collected the headless chicken upside-down by its feet and sunk it deep into a five gallon pail of boiling water. She dunked it in and out several times and then timed it for five minutes. It really did reek as it lay in the pail, headless and drenched, and I turned my delicate nose up in disgust. There certainly was nothing pleasant about this job. Five minutes elapsed and Mother tied the chicken up with binder twine to the nail on the old porch. I can still see the wretched animal strung there, taken without its consent.

I started plucking, tearing away at the soggy feathers as fast as I could, and revealing a tender, pink body. As it slowly emerged, so did the bumps on the skin. It was hard to work your way around the body and get into the folds on the chicken legs. Mother always reprimanded me for being too quick to finish. The pinfeathers still hung from the body and little fuzzes stayed embedded in the flesh. The older I got the more patience I had and the more careful I became. At the end of this step, we would take a candle to the small feathers that were left and singe them off. This was my favourite part.

The last step belonged to Mother. She could eviscerate like no other. Her precise cuts drew open the innards of the chicken. I would liken her unto a surgeon. That is just how good she was. The insides where still warm and she would explain what each part was as we went along. The gall bladder had a little sack on it that would poison the whole chicken if it wasn't taken out properly. She saved the heart, liver and the neck; the rest went to the dog or the trash. This process repeated itself fifty times over. That's how many chickens we had each year.

COZYNESS

Night would come, the end to another day. I would kneel down by the side my bed and pray, trying to speak the appropriate phrase so that something about life would make sense. I don't think I ever got it right because life remained mediocre at best. For me the best part of the day was climbing under the covers and feeling the heaviness of the blankets against my body. It felt so, so good to just lie there and soak up the warmth. I read for a while which brought me to a place of groggy delight. Soon I was out for the night. Slumber took its toll as I sank into my pillow and wrapped the covers tightly around me. In the winter, Mother would put on extra blankets in the middle of the night. It was especially cold and Father worked until dawn to get the furnace going once again. It went out a lot as I remember.

NIGHT SHIVERS

I sat up quickly, unable to breath. It had come once again, catching me unawares. The room was dark, almost eerily so. I jumped out of bed, panic-stricken. I tried to find some light but the black, cold room hemmed me in. The moon that usually shone in my window was down low that night bringing no hope of salvation. I could hear my sister breathing quietly across the room. Her even breathing was like the steady ticking of a clock. At least something, someone was alive and well.

I closed my eyes tight, trying to forget, but I couldn't. I was running and running, tripping and falling, then getting up and running some more, too afraid to look behind, I traveled at a faster pace. Nothing could keep me from getting away from the looming figure behind. A panicked whisper constricted my throat. The words would not come out. I needed help and reassurance that I would be OK. Just OK, that's all I wanted to be.

This looming stranger was not new to me. He came most every night, bringing terror and darkness. Sometimes he was dressed as my brother, sometimes as my Father. Just the thought of looking straight into his eye created a shadow of threat. Why I felt the need to run from him was unknown to me. He was a common, everyday person.

I threw my legs over the side of the bed, feeling a wisp of the refreshing coolness of the room. I was on automatic, and I started rocking back and forth with my body, deeply and slowly. What other choice did I have? My arms crossed over each other, squeezed tightly, trying to soothe my blackened soul. No one was there to rescue me; I would have to deal with this one on my own, like I did with most other things in my short life. The aloneness of it all was almost embarrassing. How could it be so real yet remain a mystery? It was all I knew and as far as I could tell, all I would ever know.

Eventually, the small room came into focus. I could see into the shadowy night and a few features of the room stood out. The sparkly linoleum floor with its worn cracks came into view. I tried to read the covers of the books that were kept on the dark brown shelves across the room. Little trinkets lined the shelves, creating an awkward attempt at beauty. I found the tiny closet in the corner that held our small wardrobes. The frosted windowpane reaching out into a big world gave me a measure of hope. They all added to my picture of reality. Slowly the fear subsided; I climbed back under my pink flowered covers and buried my head into the sweet smell of my flannel sheets. Concentrating on my roommate's slow, even breathing; I fell into a deep sleep, with a deep consciousness that the nightmare might return.

DRIVING VACATIONS

Quite a bit of my childhood is a blur. However, some of the things cannot help but stand out. One of those things is holidays. My Father was always happy. He still got up at 6 am in the morning to go walking. I am not sure walking is the word for it, more like slow-pace jogging. He had seen half the world while the rest of us slept snugly in our cots.

We had graduated from tent to tent-trailer to trailer all in the matter of a few years. This was my Father's excuse to buy bigger and bigger vehicles with more horsepower. Mother was happy with each new step because it meant less work for her. Looking back, I can see now why she sat out on so many of the ventures. Those peaceful moments gave her the energy to go on. She was often tired, worn out, and much too old before her time.

We went on many vacations as a family. My personal favourite was Disney World in Florida. The drive down there was something else. Each state had its own accent and way of treating a Canadian, especially Georgia. As soon as the inhabitants heard that we were from Canada, they would start in on a long questioning period. Sometimes we could hardly understand them for their accents.

"I didn't know you drove cars."

"Where's your Eskimo parka?"

"How cold does it get in your igloo at night?"

"How far can you go on your dog sled?"

"Do you trap bear and moose?"

"Don't you have snow all year round?"

On and on the questions went until our minds were reeling and our eyes were rolling. Underneath the straight face, there was a big snicker about to come out but somehow we always managed to keep ourselves in line. The mountain of questions went on and on, almost bringing us to our knees in laughter.

There were other momentous occasions on the highway in Georgia too. The traffic, one day, had come to a fizzling halt. We were moving so slowly it felt like we were leaning towards backwards. Father had been driving for almost four hours and was getting tired of the monotony. He felt there was no way of getting out of the car to switch drivers. So we came up with this brilliant plan as a family. My little brother always sat in the front between my Mother and Father so it was easy to climb over him. The question was who would steer the car while the switch was taking place. Keith always sat behind Father, so he slid his hand gingerly onto the wheel and tried to direct the car straight down the road while the switch took place. I was right in the center of the car enjoying my place in the middle. We laughed, giggled, and wondered if this would actually work. It all went smoothly, without a hitch and Mother was in the driver's seat before we knew it. And the Georgians wondered if we could drive cars! We could even do tricks with them.

I believe it was on a Floridian beach close to Disney World. I was beat from Father's frantic pace. So I decided to climb underneath a beach lounger for and rest for the afternoon. Soon the lull of the waves took their toll and put me into a deep sleep. Everything around me was lost, as I lay motionless on the sand unknowing of what was to come. I am sure my brothers played Frisbee and my sister lay in the shade and read. The scorching sun beat down upon my back and while others lathered the sunscreen on over and over, I lay unknowingly on the sandy beach in a dreamy, blissful state. Since my head was under the lounger, I did not feel the heat pouring down on my back with a powerful force.

After a day of play at the white, sandy beach, my eyes opened with a start at Mother's voice. "Let's go for supper now," she said. It was obvious she had been in the shade for her voice was happy from a day of rest. I, on the other hand, was groggy and a little afraid to move. I began to feel the crunchy, baked feeling on my back. It slowly ran down my legs into the bottoms of my feet. Soon my family stood around me, laughing as though I were a baked lobster fresh from the kill. I groaned inwardly, which brought stabbing pain to my back; I was cooked, baked, and broiled.

Trying to move my head out from under the chair promptly brought more pain by bonking me on the head. I slowly rose to my feet and when I finally reached an upright position; my brother decided whacking me on the back would be funny. A jolt of lightning zapped against my skin. The pain was electrifying. I cried out as loud as I could for effect, then lunged at Keith in fury. I was completely incensed at his audacity. This behaviour must be retaliated against. I swung every which way with my hands never quite within reach of his back, or any other part of his body for that matter. It was all a rather large lesson in futility.

The crunching in my shoulders only brought further discomfort. It wasn't long before Mother's voice rang out, "Enough you two, it's time to get going." So just as I turned away in obedience Keith got me again. I didn't believe that my back could have turned any redder but my face sure did. As I dove for one more good wallop, Mother almost shrieked at me. There was no way to return Keith's favour. I would have to wait for a more appropriate time.

I did develop quite the case of sunstroke lying on that beach. But I suffered a stroke of a different kind in the next segment of my childhood. It seemed that water and I got along famously. Wherever it was, I went. I followed it and it followed me. Every vacation you would see me climbing as close as I could to the water's edge and exploring what was deep down inside the cool, clear rivers and lakes. Since I went on quite a few of these vacations as a child to Yellowstone, Arizona, Florida, Banff, you name it – there was always one more wondrous water system to explore.

One very fine and warm day, I dared to climb up and over a huge boulder, and "deftly" landed on the other side. I dangled my blue canvas shoes in the swift current, enjoying the coolness and the sense of wellbeing it gave me. For some odd reason I always felt at one with creation in moments like these. The sun was intensely warm on my back. I listened to the ripple of the water pleasantly splashing along. There couldn't be a better moment in time.

I have no one to blame but myself for what happened next: A sudden surge in the currents, much stronger than all the others, caught hold of my blue canvas shoe and stole it right off of my foot. I watched with shock and horror as it rushed away.

I was uncertain of the depth of the water so that counted out diving in after it; besides, the water was unpleasantly cold. Instead, I yelled for help. Father, who was much more aware of the repercussions of a lost shoe than I was, came to my rescue. Adjusting his goggles properly over his face, he lunged down underneath the icy water; he came up with a small round mirror a minute or two later. It was chipped around the edges. It had been under the depths of the water but when he brought it out the mirror became a completely different colour. It was a treasure all right, but not the one we were looking for.

He dove down again, this time with more force. It was clear this was going to take some adrenaline to produce that holey, canvas shoe. This time he came up with someone else's shoe; it was for the same foot as I was already wearing. This just wouldn't do. He straightened his goggles and then groaned. He gave me a sort of quizzical look, half way between exasperation and pleasure.

By now, the whole family had joined in to watch my dilemma. Keith had jumped into the water with Father to show off his immense prowess as a man. Joy stood there with her nose up in the air. She was never surprised by my constant stupidity. It was as though she had known I was going to mess up before I ever did. My lack of proper etiquette caused her to rejoice. Her arms were crossed, waiting to hear the somber news that my shoe was lost forever.

Andy was Andy. He was always laughing so it wasn't hard to tell what his response would be. Crystal clear fits of laughter rippled through the small gorge. Mother snuck up on the lot of us, her head shaking slowly from side to side. The words, "Not again!" were written all over her face. She was never sure what to do with me at the best of times. She just stood there, unmoving like a stone statue.

I turned towards the river, intent on the prolonged rescue effort. Father was down below in the clear blue water. Keith was trying to be handy by diving in and out of the frigid water. He usually came up with a hand full of stones, not that useful but, nevertheless, an attempt. Father was growing weary. The water was beyond freezing and both Keith and Father had red, red skin dotted with shivery bumps. Although I cannot remember the final item Father dredged out of the water I know it was not my blue canvas shoe. All my hopes were dashed. We were the prizewinners of a chipped round mirror. Well, at least I had one shoe. I didn't really know if it that was better than none but I was about to discover the reality of living WITH only one.

I left that park in solitude, wandering in shock over the escapade. My scattered family walked on ahead, each with their own thoughts. I waited for Father to say he would go find a shoe store and restore my feet to some sense of normalcy. But no such words came from his lips. As we reached the blue Ford LTD, he reached out his arm towards my shoulder. My thought of that shopping trip was renewed but instead he stated that I would have to walk around with one shoe for the rest of the trip. I blinked back the tears that quickly welled up in my eyes. I couldn't understand why there wouldn't be enough money to buy a $5 pair of shoes. Yet the word was spoken and there would be no sense in challenging Father's decision. Maybe we could sell the mirror and raise money somehow. I knew that thought was useless, but I had it nevertheless. I was thus relegated to walking with one shoe the rest of the trip.

We drove away with Father already dreaming up his next adventure. When we got to the caves, I couldn't go in. I believe it was the Carlsbad Caverns so maybe we were in South Dakota. None of the actual destinations stand out in my mind. With one shoe, it was impossible to struggle up and down the cavern rock. The dark, wet surface was not meant for my feet to walk on. I was told later there was one huge stalactite that actually created a stalagmite on the bottom of the cave.

I was thoroughly depressed, sitting on a blasted bench with Mother. She had her legs crossed casually, looking out across the park landscape. She was fully enthralled with the forest surroundings. A warm breeze blew gently along. The vacationers walking by were happy. Little children wandered aimlessly along, enjoying the weather, jumping over rocks. The long-needled pine trees created a plethora of greens, too many to count. Mother was satisfied with just looking out over the tree line.

I did not understand this, especially when there were new frontiers right in front of us to be explored. It was beyond my comprehension. Time went slowly. Mother said we could not walk around because we didn't know when THEY might come out of THE CAVE. There was that word again. I fumbled with my fingers, rocked back and forth swinging my legs around; it was no use, they weren't coming, they would never come.

When they finally did arrive, they were giddy with laughter. Their tour guide had cracked jokes left and right. The beauty of the cave had been incredible. They used every adjective in the book while I sat on that darned bench, listening with half an ear. If I had to hear one more word about how rapturous that cave was, I was going to throw up. I climbed off the bench and marched away. I could not take it anymore, enough of that racket. Of course, I didn't get very far before I was called back and it was time to go. Off we went the six of us, one big happy family, off to discover yet another of God's creations.

Vacations made Father into a different person. He was a pleasure to be around. Nothing disturbed his carefree demeanour. We went to Disney World several times and I am sure that Father was just as much of a kid as all the rest of us were. He stood in the long lineups for the rides, talking to anybody that went by. He bought us Fudgsicles and useless souvenirs. He tried to cajole Mother into being happy, which never really worked. He dragged us along on every adventure he had discovered by reading tourist guides before we left home. There was no stopping him.

WALT'S WONDER

On one trip to this divinely entertaining place called Disney World, our parents thought us old enough to be divided into pairs and left to our own course of action. That meant Andy and I were on our own. I was the older of the two at a whopping nine years of age but we did not complain. We had no particular plan but went from ride to ride, whatever struck our fancy in the moment.

Some lineups had signs clearly stating that the wait would be an hour long. At first, we adhered to these lineup rules with tenacity. But the further along into the day we got, the braver we got. We ducked under the ropes, winding our way through a maze of people, to get through the line faster. The little old ladies laughed at us, declaring us cute. But the middle-aged, impatient men, who could do nothing about their plight, threatened to call the authorities. This only caused us to push on down the line faster than ever before. We thought it was great fun and usually reached our final destination in ten minutes instead of the long hour proposed at the beginning of the line.

The sound of the Disney song "It's a Small World after all" still drums in my head. I swore I would never subject myself to it again but I went the next time the opportunity presented itself. On one ride, we stood on this huge elevator with headless beings appearing around us and freaky voices declaring we would never get out of the deep cavern we were about to enter. There were screeches and wails surrounding us as we climbed aboard our black carriage. Lightning flashed, thunder crashed, evil laughter shook us in our seats. Our carriage twisted backwards and we slid down a long hill in terror, wondering what would come next. Freaked beyond recognition, we came out into the open air, ready to go again. Space Mountain wasn't open yet so we settled for a monstrous outdoor rollercoaster. Dipping and diving along, screaming to our hearts' content, we had the thrill of a lifetime. "Twenty Thousand Leagues under the Sea", with its obviously fake sea creatures floating aimlessly under water, was a bit of a downer after all that excitement.

We stopped for lunch at a street vendor and we coughed up just enough change for two hot dogs and a Coke. Food was not what we had come for. Sitting on a wooden bench in the middle of the square, we watched Mickey Mouse, Donald Duck and other

Disney characters roam around, bringing good cheer to toddlers and Mothers alike. We were to meet our parents back at the Disney Castle at four o'clock so we had little time to spare. The Swiss Family Robinson tree house was next on our agenda. We climbed up high on the swinging rope ladder and gazed out at the wonderful world of Disney in awe and wonder.

Without a cloud in the sky and no sunscreen, we played our way through the rest of the afternoon. Our feet where growing weary, but we pressed on deciding another ride in the haunted mansion would be our final event. By the time we reached the big Disney castle in the middle of this world of wonder it was a little past four. Our six- and eight-year-old bodies sank down on the closest bench and rested from our wild adventures. As the rest of the family arrived, we sauntered back to the car rejoicing in the wonder of the day.

THE SCHOOL SPELLING BEE

Every school year, the segments of time were exactly the same, broken down by report cards, Christmas break, spring break, track and field and last but not least the municipal Spelling Bee. I cannot say I ever really understood grammar, but I could spell like a maniac. In grade four I came ever so close to winning the school Bee and in grade five, I won. This meant I was off to an even bigger competition with better competitors.

Mother made sure I looked my best by sewing me a bright red, Fortrel suit. The top had big brass buttons all the way down with huge white lapels. The skirt was far too short for my comfort. I'm not sure what Mother had been thinking when she sewed it. I sat in the back seat of the white Mercury Marquis as my nerves shook. I kept trying to pull my skirt over my knees, thankful at least that I would be standing at the Spelling Bee.

I never once looked out into the audience as I spelled the words given to me. I wasn't shy about spelling loudly and clearly, as long as I pretended I was at home in my room alone. Standing before the crowd was too much for me to think about. Never in my life would I have envisioned myself a star.

When the whole thing was over and I was waiting for the results all I could think about was getting home as quickly as possible. Hearing my name called for first place almost caused me a heart attack. I was sure some mistake had been made. When asked to come forward to receive the trophy, I had to accept that this was for real. I had won the spelling contest.

Mrs. Penner treated me like a queen the next day at school. She smiled at me with pleasure and delight. I did my best to smile back but I felt more like glaring. The whole class got cake to celebrate my victory. Everyone shared in my glory. I didn't really know what to do with all this positive reinforcement. It was a shock to my system. I was glad when the day was over and everything went back to normal...until the next year that is.

Spelling Bee competition time came around again. Only this time there was no contest in our little school. Mrs. Penner sent me off to the Spelling Bee, without even so much as a discussion, to the sad dismay of all my friends. Some of them wouldn't even talk to me. I was soon relegated to a small space under the cement stairs at the back of the school for noon recess. Being alone wasn't all that bad but what I couldn't stand was all the whispering behind my back. Mrs. Penner had succeeded in making my life a living hell.

I went to the Bee that year because that was what was expected of me but I cannot say I participated wholeheartedly. In the very end when there were just a few of us left I decided to put an end to this foolishness. I purposely spelled the word "reindeer" wrong. Nobody was the wiser and I was free to go back to life as usual. Mrs. Penner was not smiling at me the next day as I walked in the class and I have to say that her grim expression was a great relief to me.

TV AND CURLERS

It was the sound of the television that calmed me down after the Spelling Bee. Between Lawrence Welk and Sonny and Cher, I forgot all my woes. Little Charity Bono was so cute and you could do nothing but laugh at the nutty dances on the Lawrence Welk show. Watching these shows seemed to be a Saturday night tradition with us, at least in the winter.

The only perturbing part of this ritual was Mother trying to put a brush and comb through my hair. She cared for nothing more than to get done as quickly as possible. The torment did not end with the brushing. Then came the curlers. They were hard, silver-coloured metal. My hair was so thick; it took her forever to get done. I wriggled and fussed. Every two minutes I was asking if we were done yet. Mother had little patience and forced me down on the couch with her hands, trying to keep me still. The only consolation was that I had beautiful ringlets to show off at church in the morning.

Sleeping on a head of metal every Saturday night was not my idea of fun. I would toss and turn, trying to find a comfortable position. One time, I stole a few of the curlers from the back of my head and lay down on the flat part. Although Mother was not particularly pleased in the morning, it allowed me some semblance of sleep.

Besides getting to watch television as a family on Saturday night, we also got to create our own special dessert. During the day I would bake my famous chocolate cake. It always turned out deep brown with a moistness that made your mouth water. There were red cherries, sometimes green, vanilla ice cream, chocolate sauce, sometimes caramel and last but not least, whipped cream to die for. There was always a big fight about who would go first. The lines we formed became more of a snake-like form. We dove in and out, between arms, over heads. We shoved and pushed each other, half laughing, half angry. Mother and Father watched from their chairs waiting patiently for their turn. They never interrupted the scene, nor scolded us for our foolishness. I suppose we were just too entertaining to watch.

Sitting down on the couch, relishing that first bite, was heaven. Bringing the spoon close to my mouth activated the saliva glands. The first spoonful would slide in. The tastes and textures would strike my tongue, they were absolutely glorious. Rapture had definitely occurred. I would nurse the concoction to death in my mouth. Both brothers would inhale theirs and go for seconds. I figured the pure pleasure of the experience was worth it all.

'TIS THE SEASON

Christmas started out with the same routine every year. Father would bring the ancient decorations out from the musty basement. The smell carried throughout the house for a while but with time, the beauty of the ornaments would flourish and take on the smells of Christmas. Maybe a scented cinnamon candle was burning somewhere close by or perhaps the creation of scrumptious Christmas baking, in all its glory, was being prepared for the holiday festivities. Either way, the musty smell would disappear, and the glitter of the ornaments would take over.

I was the one who decorated the tree and I loved it, a prized position, I thought. I wielded my magic with the many strings of lights. They were multi-coloured and huge by today's standards.

Father would ready the fake, old tree for me. He would connect the pieces, bending the branches back and forth. I always felt sorry for the artificial limbs as they were pushed and prodded into their proper place until they looked like some semblance of a tree. I would rearrange every stiff branch until it took on a life of its own.

The decorations were so shiny and pretty. The delicate glass balls glowed with a white dust that had been sprinkled on them in the factory. The glass birds were iridescent with long stiff, white tail feathers fanning out behind. The soft, glittery garland wound its way around and around, sparkling like the morning sun. I would fling the flimsy icicles carelessly here and there, filling out barren spots. Finally, the golden Christmas star would be placed at the top. I would stretch and stretch to reach to the very top tip of the tree. Giving up, I would get a chair from the dining room. Climbing atop the wobbly old chair, I would finish my masterpiece off by carefully setting the star, the signature piece, on the very top of my creation. It looked precarious and heavenly all at once. My work of beauty was complete and now I could sit back, satisfied.

Christmas Eve was the best. When early evening rolled around, Mother would shoo us all out of the house and we would wait forever in the car, laughing and carrying on. She must have been making last-minute preparations for our celebration after the service at church. She hurried out the door with a soft smile on her face. I became curious, flushed with excitement. Something wonderful was up but as hard as I tried I couldn't figure it out. We drove to our little church with Mother chattering on about how Santa had come and she had to give him cookies and milk for the rest of his long journey flying through the sky. There wasn't a doubt in my mind that her words were the utmost truth. I was mesmerized by Christmas. She could have told me anything. It was just plain good to see her happy.

I wiggled all the way through the intolerably long service. It was festive, I'll give it that. There was lots of singing: "Hark the Herald Angels Sing" and other long Christmas songs with too many verses to count.

Sparkly decorations where hung everywhere. The manger scene lay softly as a centerpiece at the front of the sanctuary. Baby Jesus looked so sweet and innocent in His Kingly cradle, his face full of the promise of new life.

None of this Christmas wonder stopped the jiggles and jitters of the night from growing ever bigger. I wanted to be home again to see the treasures Santa had brought on his sleigh. We kids raced out to the car with our yearly brown paper bags of candy, oranges, chewy licorice, and peanuts. The parents were not waiting in the car at the end of the service. We stuffed our faces voraciously while Mother and Father took their jolly time visiting with friends, conspiratorial smirks on their faces. As they sauntered out of the church door, we tried to look unsuspecting of the things to come.

The home front was in sight now. Speed was of the essence. But instead, Father took his jolly time driving home, declaring it was too icy to go faster. We dawdled along while Mother asked us questions about the service. The answers came quickly even though I had paid attention to very little. It was as though I had sucked it up by osmosis. As we reached the farmyard driveway, my heart was pumping wildly.

Once inside the door, toppling over each other, faces spread with glee, we raced into the living room for a peek at the presents under the tree. Sure enough, Santa had come again while we were out. I went around touching and poking each present trying to figure out which one was mine. I was sure I had found it when a hand grabbed me from behind. I wasn't to touch the presents, only look and dream. The waiting was not over, for now the Christmas story began.

Father sat in his navy blue armchair and read aloud from the Bible, all about Mary and Joseph and baby Jesus. I closed my eyes in earnest, trying hard to concentrate. Mother was just as antsy as the rest of us. Her eyes gave away her inner secrets. She loved watching us open our presents one by one, and thought Father dragged out the biblical reading far too long. But she never said anything although there where the crossed arms and tapping feet to tell us her impatience in getting on with it. I think she simply imagined herself as one of the children.

Andy was Santa's helper and handed out the presents one by one. We all took turns opening our presents so each could admire the others take. Now this was Mother's idea and Keith was usually last. He had extra-long to wait before finding out what Father and Mother had gotten him for Christmas.

But it was never long before the bright wrapping paper was demolished and the cherished toys were held in our chubby little hands. The macaroons and rosebuds with red and green shiny wrappers appeared magically from behind Father's chair. The chocolate macaroons were my favourite and I dug into the bag by the handful. I hoped that no one would see my sticky, brown hands and the smile that was a telltale sign I had ingested too much chocolate.

We played with the new toys that had sat in their Christmas wrappings for so long. It seemed to me that this was the one time of year that Mother and Father where both happy. They tried to make the day special for us and they succeeded.

CHRISTMAS RELATIVES

Christmas affairs were long and drawn out in our house. There was this relative and that relative that came to visit. Then we would travel three hours each way every year to celebrate with Mother's side of the family. The further we went away from Winnipeg the more scenic the terrain became. Hills and lakes appeared and I strained to see wildlife out of the car window.

There was a rule in the car; no one could touch anyone else in the cramped back seat of the car. I sat in the middle on the hard hump of the seat, forcing my body into an awkward position so as not to upset Keith and Joy. Arriving at Mother's oldest brother's house after the three-hour car ride, I toppled out of the car, balancing my body until it finally stood upright. It was a relief to feel life being forced back into my long limbs as I stretched and moved.

I saw my uncle Hal. He was my favourite at these functions. There were three younger uncles who told joke after joke, trying to outdo each other, but he always took the prize. The older uncles were solemn and morose, even at Christmas. Uncle Hal was really the only uncle who paid quality attention to his nieces and nephews and he stole my heart.

We would all gather together in what was a not-so-big living room, most of us kids sitting on the floor, legs crossed. For a while, it was the adults and the children together but eventually the children grew bored with the adult conversation, and we scampered away to various parts of the big old farm. I was closest to my cousin Geoffrey and we had a blast together. Sometimes he got a little rough but I did not admit to that since I usually applied the first playful hit.

My aunt and uncle had a massive hayloft, perfect for playing hide and seek. Since there were at least thirty cousins, adventure in the bales of hay was crazy and wild. We set the loft up so that there were plenty of hiding places. There were deep holes, long bridges, wobbly towers, and narrow walkways, all made out of bales. After setting up the bales, we would all scatter to find our hiding places.

The oldest child always went first to try to find the younger cousins. Finding someone meant that person was added to the search party. This meant that by the end, the majority of the cousins were searching for the few remaining hidden ones. It became a challenge to remain still enough so no one could find you, especially since it was cold out. Breathing out gave a clue to where someone was hidden. So we had to be extra careful not to let our breath show while we were hiding. There were no prizes or trophies for the last one to be found, just the thrill of having beaten them all the others.

Before long, it was time for Christmas dinner. My oldest aunt, who had the same name my Mother did, would call out the door of the old farmhouse and we would be off. We never took the easy way out. It was either jump out of the loft window to our death below or climb down the baler, the long conveyer belt. This was my personal favourite. Climbing between the tines was a true challenge. They were sharp and unruly and being stabbed by just one tine brought droplets of blood to tender skin. The width of the frame was far too long for my legs so I had to reach and strain with all my might to get from one rung to another. Geoffrey laughed at me as he flew by through the air, landing in a pile of cow dung; his Mother wouldn't be happy with him for carrying in such a mess on Christmas day.

We trampled dirt and hay in through the porch first and then throughout the house. We were tired and hungry after all our hard work playing in the barn. Since there were so many of us, Mother had six brothers and a sister, we couldn't all sit at the table. We kids got that place of honour at the table while the adults sat in the living room with TV trays.

It was buffet style so we all rushed to the counter to see who could be first. I had some lanky cousins who always won the race. This also meant that half the food was gone by the time I got there. Every aunt had prepared something. There were so many colours of salads: red, pink, green and this incredible purple Jell-o salad that left your mouth watering for more. However, the steaming turkey was my personal favourite. Turkey was more than a leftover to me. Its savoury smell overwhelmed my taste buds and created comfort in my belly before I even had eaten any of it. The gravy, stuffing and potatoes added just the right combination, creating warmth and pleasure deep within.

Now, you had to be tough to make it through the food line. You where jostled this way and that, pushed forward as someone took a fork from you and started in on your precious turkey. I don't know how many birds my aunt cooked but it was certainly more than one. Then it was back to the festively decorated table to tell jokes, stuff our faces and spread laughter all around. There was never any fighting, just joyous frivolity. This was the one time of year we got to see each other and no one was about to spoil it.

Eventually the group of relatives broke up to play card games or catch up on some home front news. I followed my girl cousins into Gail's bedroom. They were pretending to be nurses and doctors, making plastic dolls come alive by moving arms and legs and twisting heads this way and that. I joined in the fun, sitting down on the floor. We gave the dolls their medicine and injections. We gave them intravenous drugs as a part of hospital protocol.

My doll's name was Gracie and she was wearing a deep blue dress. She had lost her socks and shoes long ago but she was still pretty all the same. Her hair was slightly matted from the many times the comb had been pulled through it. I think it was supposed to be curly but it had gone extra frizzy instead.

I tried to concentrate on beautifying my doll, but couldn't help noticing something unusual was happening in a small corner of the rectangular room. I tried to ignore it by putting different clothing on my doll, but the dresses looked awkward and were all too big.

Gail was now asking my cousin Jill, ever so politely, if she would come play a game with her. The first thing she was to comply with was to get naked by unzipping her pants. Although Jill was confused by this request, she quickly whisked off her clothing. Gail was a big bully and Jill knew it. The bruises she would inflict in secret would be worse than any twisted game Gail wanted to play now.

Her next request grew even more bizarre. Jill was to lie perfectly still on the twin bed in the room. It was Gail's bed, of course. There was a sense that it had been used for such games before. Gail hovered over her, declaring her doctoral ability. She was not the least bit embarrassed by her behaviour, but I was. It shocked me, as she pulled her fingers in and out of Jill's very private place. I was terrified. I drew a deep breath. Horror penetrated my soul. The motion haunted me.

Gail now declared that she was the doctor and all the rest of us were her patients. The problem was, I was an unwilling patient. I was paralyzed. She was my older and much bigger cousin. I should trust her; certainly, she would not do anything to harm me.

I was next, right after Jill. I was shaking as I walked gingerly over to the bed. I did not want to look into her face. Her eyes seemed sinister to me. She was getting some bizarre, twisted pleasure out of all of this. I did as she commanded, all the while closing my eyes tight as I pulled down my pants. The only act of defiance I could think of was to move slow and steady, not faltering in light of her stern demeanour, but I knew what was required of me so I compliantly lay down on the bed. I lay with my arms straight by my side, stiff like a board.

The routine was the same. She explained that she was checking things out in case there were any medical concerns. A foreign object pressed down hard against me, making me feel like vomiting all over the pretty, ruffled sheets and blanket. Things in the room began to disappear.

Her response was cold and gleeful, as if I liked the procedure and she had not inflicted pain on me. In fact, she had a smile of utmost pleasure on her face. I remained confused, but there was nothing to do but lie perfectly still until the process was complete.

Finally, she took soap and washed me clean. I really don't know why. When she was finished with all of us, she declared it all one big secret. I never doubted her. I felt disrespected, ashamed of myself. How had I let this happen? I dulled myself for the rest of the day. There was no longer any celebration left in me. I felt that I would never be the same. I prayed as hard as I could that my memory of this medical exam would disappear from reality.

My mind was swirling. I had come to expect the worst from life. Feelings of despair took control. I felt battered, bruised deep within. No matter how hard I tried I could not drag myself beyond the complete despair of the day. Yet another secret had found its way into my already dark reality. I was tired of being used, and growing old quickly at the age of 11.

Was I the only one being treated with such disdain, such disrespect? My body seemed to belong to everyone but me. My tormentors took over and I became a slave to their darkness. I was tired of putting up defenses. My walls were slowly crumbling into nothing. I needed to find an oasis, a source of refreshment. But try as I might, searching within my mind, there was no way out of the pain. The cruelty of abuse had taken its toll on my small life. My spirits were dampened. I lost all hope of ever regaining a semblance of normalcy.

THE LAST JOURNEY

I took the knife and cut, I cut deep into my skin, finding the richest artery, knowing I would die. The water was warm, a little too warm, but that did not matter. As I stepped into it, I saw the deep red blood flow out of my wrist. The knife was by my side as I slid down into the tub, relishing the warmth and the scarlet colour of the water.

I took the knife and sliced into my other wrist, waiting for the life to flow from me. I eyed the water to see if the colour would become even more seductive, and it did. I was completely controlled by the morbidity of my soul. Nothing and no one could stop me from the complete enjoyment of this moment. Nobody could take away the deep sense of joy and the soothing peace. I was to be comforted at last. The emptiness would be gone.

I slid into a deep sleep. No one could harm me. No one would misunderstand. They would flog themselves for not hearing my cry. And I, I would cry out into the darkness no more. The empty echo of silence, the morbid fear of being annihilated would no longer chase me relentlessly. I would have what I most deeply desired at last, complete, peace, openness, freedom. I would no longer need, and no longer be misread. Nothing would clutch me in its power. No one would grip my soul and strip me of self. No longer could anyone enter unheeded into my world, control my inner life. I would be complete, set apart from my world.

I would be free from the deafening scream of rage resounding in my soul, free from the insane demand to be whole. The search for contentment would be in the past. The snapshot of despair in my mind would stop developing. I would no longer be controlled by a cycle of desire, desperation, and then emptiness. The feeling of having something so near yet never within my grasp would be gone. It would not own me, I would own it.

I stand back and weep, the emptiness returns as I slide back into this world, another failed attempt. As the blood and the water mix, the water takes on a different hue. I have not cut deeper into my skin. 1 am puzzled. A stream of deep, pure, rich blood is pouring over mine. The picture is grim, frightful, death to bring life? The blood offering mixes together with my own tarnished blood. Life offered.

I watch from afar as His huge frame picks me up out of the water, hovering over me, oh, so close. My wrists are covered over by His massive hands. He binds up my self-made wounds. A stifled groan falls from my lips. I am so thirsty, so parched. The blood flow returns to my veins, bringing new life. Death comes so close. Jesus comes closer. He offers to dwell with me, surrounded by dark waters. It brings a savoured sense of release. Darkness cannot stop this Saviour.

LOST IN SHADOW

Dying was a thought that was ever close as a child. During those arduous years of growing up, thoughts of ending my small life grew rampant, but only to me, hidden to others. On one of many days, all the same to me, one of the things I feared the most happened over again. He came up behind me, startling me. I was pushed down those old basement stairs like a rag doll. I could hardly stand upright as I went down each step, but it was not an option. Swaying back and forth I fell into the frozen depths.

The figure behind me loomed large in my mind. He made sure all the lights were out. There was only one small window in this damp cell. I did not know why seeing it was so important anyway. The only thing that changed in his management of the situation was the placement of the bruises. He was taller and stronger than I so there didn't seem to be much sense in fighting back. He laughed as he slapped and kicked me as hard as he could. One set of bashes after another left me feeling dizzy.

His timing was impeccable. All were out of my reach and hearing distance. At first, I did try to fight back. However, my feeble pushes and shoves made little difference. It was almost as if I digressed off my path of trying to overthrow him, just giving up. It was beyond impossible to stop him, he was an immoveable force.

Finally, he twisted both arms behind my back. Holding my two wrists in one hand, he forced me to the ground. I had lost the battle. He tied my hands together and then tied them to the grey basement pole. I slouched down the cold pole onto my knees, exhausted from the fight. I knew I would be here until one of my parents came home.

He left, feeling elated at his power. I only felt helpless and alone, so I closed my eyes and drifted into a faraway land. There were princesses and dragons (only the good kind), green forests brought about fullness of life. My dreams were kept alive as long as I kept my eyes tightly shut. There was no longer fear of any pain...at least until the next time.

I lay on the damp floor, my body growing weary from its awkward pose. Even with the promise of the green blue bruises scattered over my body, I did not cry. After all, this was a way of life for me. He made me promise to keep it a secret or the beating would be worse the next time. This was an intentional threat I knew he would keep. No one would know of the deep, dark path I had to embrace. It was to be held in the strictest confidence, and I would keep my part of the bargain.

My thoughts grew frantic. I could see no way of ever entering into any of the closeness that I longed for. I was heartbroken on the inside. I felt sad and alone. My gut told me I wasn't safe here in this house. But my mind tried to be safe, it tried to fit in, belong. Nobody could see inside me. Nobody seemed to care either. I was trapped in my small body and sorely ashamed of any feelings I had of wanting to be loved. They only led me to a dark cavern. I was certain nothing but carnage lay there. I would wander aimlessly looking for a way out, but none would be found. My feet were raw and bleeding from stumbling along the cold, hard rocks. My knees showed a bruised, yellowy tint made brighter and brighter with each fall. All I knew was that I was never going to make it out of here. I was lost and alone.

ESCAPE TO THE WOODS

"Who will tell whether one happy moment of love or the joy of breathing or walking on a bright morning and smelling fresh air, is not worth all the suffering and effort which life implies."

Erich Fromm

It is a curious thing, this act of living. One moment wholeness prevails, the next a sense of entrapment and deprivation. My mind willed the memory of this blight to return, to come into the light, but self-protection loomed large. I saw flashes come out of the blindness. There were heavy ropes lying on the cold cement floor. Suddenly the scene changed, bringing a surreal fear of the sudden pressure being placed on my tiny body. Scene after scene flashed in and out of my consciousness until the weight of these events overcame me.

The thing I feared was all-consuming, I ran as far and fast as I could, trying not to care what came behind me. If only I could outrun this unknown monster. The pounding of my heart grew loud in my ears. I tried to ignore it and ran on. But it felt like my heart would come right out of my body. I could see the hedge up ahead and knew it would bring safety. I was so intent on the safety of the bushes ahead of me that I forgot to look down at the uneven ground around me and lost my balance. My ankle twisted and I stumbled, perilously, down to the ground, falling flat, my face buried in the lawn. I froze for a moment and then the fear rushed in. I couldn't let this happen or I wouldn't be able to go on. Ignoring the helplessness of the situation, I jumped into action and lunged at the bushes, my fervour renewed. From then on, I was on autopilot.

I escaped to the same place every time; to a place where I belonged. The grasses grew high, forming a protective barrier. Inside there was a hollow of nature waiting, a secret hiding place far away from torment. Here I could hunker down and listen to the sounds of nature.

I waited, willing the nausea away. The feeling in my stomach was stabbing, strong and steady. I lay in the bushes, wrapped in my arms.

Hands around my knees, tightly trying to push out the pain inside my soul, there was the deep dark pain of the redness on my arms and legs from trying to rip the shame out of my body. My eyes squeezed shut, so tight that it stung. The pressure exerted on my body was not helping. I was becoming more and more anxious.

Once again, in my mind, I heard the words, "Only babies cry." Taunting me, "Only babies cry." A trace of a tear fell down my cheek. It could have easily become a torrent. I stopped it in its tracks. I inhaled slowly trying to deny the death in my shaky heart.

Eventually, the sound of birds singing softly in the trees began to seep into my consciousness. I opened my eyes just a crack to see if the world of nature would offer its usual mystical reprieve. I watched monarch butterflies fluttering randomly through the air, bright red ladybugs crawling lazily along the ground. The leaves on the trees and the tall grasses were waving back and forth in the prairie wind, reminding me that not all of life was dangerous and cold.

As I concentrated on my holy habitat, a calmness slowly descended over me like the soft, gentle breeze on my face. I floated along with it, becoming unaware of the pain this life brought. I had once again stopped the confusion in its tracks; the insanity had disappeared. I had managed to trade it for some measure of peace.

But there was a price to pay: a part of my soul cut off from reality. I became invisible, unable to see the horror that ruled my life.

"Suffering has been stronger than all other teaching, and has taught me to understand what your heart used to be, I have been bent and broken, but – I hope – into a better shape."

Charles Dickens

ICY WATERS

Every Saturday night was bath night. Our bathtub was in the basement in a small, rickety room. The stairs would creak as I walked down, careful not to disturb the canning jars Mother put on them to take down at a later date. I would hold my pajamas and my pink housecoat firmly in my hand. I always wore thick grey socks too, because the basement floor was cold and dirty. There was no banister to the one side so I always stepped on the side closest to the wall. That was where all Father's farm jackets and overalls hung. It always smelled of grease and machinery. I was the third in line to take a bath. The water was not changed in between because we could not afford it. Sometimes if we were lucky, we would get a little extra hot water so we wouldn't freeze to death in the icy depths.

The door on the bathroom was clunky. It screeched against the floor as the slat of wood twisted over the door. That was referred to as locked. There was also an archaic block of wood, maybe 2"X 4" that was turned across the door and the edge of wall for extra security. Of course, anyone could get in at any time.

The old-style washing machine was in there with the tub. It was a ringer washer. Mother hated it, but to tell you the truth I loved it. I got a kick out of cranking the handle as fast as I could to ring out the clothes. We did not own a dryer, so everything was carried up the stairs to hang on the line outside. The crunchy clothes would be brought in, winter and summer; they smelled so good and fresh from the sun and the elements.

However, let me bring you back to the pleasurable experience of my bath time. I am not sure how we ever got clean. The water was always already murky when I got in. I hoped it was because the last person had used a lot of soap. I was the third child in the tub. I could never figure out why Keith got to go first because he was the dirtiest. I guess he was the biggest and the first-born. I suppose that's all it took.

I looked at the grimy water again. My hair was long back then, requiring a complete dunk. So when I would dive under the water and blow bubbles, I would be careful not to suck any water back in. I would come up for air and shampoo. Then down again to rinsing all the shampoo out of my hair. There was no such thing as conditioner in our house so my hair was always tousled and messy. By then the water would have turned completely frigid. It felt colder than the air outside of it. I would use the soap as quickly as possible, splashing the water over my body. Then I would jump out of the tub quickly, dry off and put on my fresh pajamas and pink bathrobe. Brush in hand, I would walk upstairs, careful not to rub against Father's dirty overalls.

I remember one incident clearly. With the inadequate lighting, it was always dingy in the basement and I was afraid. I could never get up the stairs quickly enough for my liking, especially when having to be careful to not knock any canning jars over on the one side and not touch the filthy work clothes on the other. I was concentrating so hard that I didn't realize my big brother was waiting for me around the corner at the top of the stairs. I opened the basement door a crack and he lunged at me, screaming in his high-pitched adolescent tone. I screamed too and ran right back down those stairs.

The dinginess of the basement was somewhat of a reprieve compared to the "brotherly love" that awaited me at the top of those long, creaky stairs. But now I was trapped between my fear of my brother and my fear of the dark basement.

Suddenly all the lights went out. I squeezed my eyes shut, imagining I was in a bright room with all the lights on. No one came to my rescue. I felt as if I would be left alone in the dingy basement forever. My brother had conquered once again. I was the weak one and he was big and strong.

Eventually Mother would tell him to quit and I would dash to the safety of the sofa, seeking comfort under a soft blanket. Mother would start raking the brush through my hair, my head being pulled this way and that. It hurt but I didn't make a sound. I had been taught not to cry out a long time ago.

Looking back on it now, it is no wonder that I don't like baths to this day.

ALL ALONE

I was a stranger in my own home with no one to understand me. But once I reached my room I felt warmth. There was no one crossing my path, and dealing with the uncomfortable struggle and strain of standing before someone, unheard and unwanted, was left behind. As hard as I tried to dislodge myself from my reality, I was paralyzed, paralyzed by the fear that this would always be the only truth in my life.

Lonely, or was it alone, was a much better place to be. I had this idea that maybe, just maybe, if I sat alone on my bed long enough I would become invisible. Nobody would hear me or see me and that is what I had tried to achieve throughout my short childhood. Growing up, reaching these horrid conclusions about this life left me tired.

It felt good to watch my parents without them noticing me. It was like watching a good program on the television. You could see into their lives, but they couldn't see you. In fact, they didn't even care. It brought a measure of safety that I felt only a few times in my life. This state of alternate reality created a pleasant, quiet cynicism towards the world as I saw it. No one could get in and I didn't want to get out.

Gaining new strength from being silent and alone, I curled up in the fetal position on the bed, wrapping my soft homemade blanket all around me, even pulling it over my head. My invisible shield was up and working. I pushed away the feeling that came over me that my cocoon wouldn't last.

This was something I had taught myself long ago, not to get caught crying, at weakness or any of sign of vulnerability. There would be no end of grief if my older brother or sister saw me crying. It just wouldn't do. So I continued my struggle and I turned the relentless memories off as quickly as they had forced themselves upon me. Numbness passed over me bringing the blessed relief of denial. I hadn't lost my touch. I truly was safe here alone in my room, all ALONE in my room.

As time moved on, I devised a plan to keep certain words from destroying my soul. Lonely and alone, dirty and ashamed, unwanted, taken advantage of - there were too many to list.

I sat up rigidly on the edge of my unmade bed looking down at the floor. It was cluttered with dirty clothes. The covers were thrown halfway down the mattress, the pillows strewn this way and that. The books that I had been reading were on my bedside table.

I always read more than one book at a time, usually becoming bored by the lack of intrigue in just one, unless of course, it was the **Archie Comics®**. These pages were well worn and dog-eared from reading them again and again.

There was one window in my room with Jack Frost expressing his creative flair for the day. The walls were full of flowers; you might say they were quite cheerful. Mostly the room was made up of two beds; that was about all that would fit in it. What else was there to do in a bedroom but sit on the bed and read anyway?

Joy and I had always had to share a room whereas Keith and Andy each got their own. For some reason, as girls we were supposed to get along better than two boys. I really didn't see the logic behind that one. We were always fighting. We only slept in the same room. Other than that we stayed out of each other's hair.

SUSTENANCE

The love of eating was one thing our whole family had in common, right down to the little Chihuahua mutt sitting patiently under the table. Mealtime was a joyous occasion. The smells emanating from the tiny farmhouse kitchen created comfortable rumbles in our stomachs. Mother slaved each day over the meal. She claimed a tall, metal stool as her own. The lines of rust embedded in the stool legs proved its age. The cracked, blue, plastic seat added a certain nostalgia from another time.

Here she plunked down her tiny frame in between tasks. She leaned her tired head against the crinkled calendar on the wall and fell into a safe doze. Sizzles and bubbles on the old, green stove were a reminder to check the various stages of delectable foods.

Joy and I each had our own designated tasks. Mine was to set the table adjacent to the kitchen. I really didn't mind it. This task was timed and nothing ever changed. Wipe the vinyl mats, set out the green, flowered Corelle, then the stained tea cups and mismatched cutlery. There was nothing pretty about it; it was a purely practical table setting.

The last-minute rush ran Mother, Joy and me off our feet. The many-coloured hot pads flying to their final resting places and then heavy, cast-iron pans plunked on top of them. Meat, potatoes and vegetables were the fare, day after day. I have to commend Mother on her creativity and ability to adhere to Father's wishes. There was little variety in our diet. Father lived on protein and carbohydrates. As the final spread was laid on the table each day, Mother bellowed repeatedly, "Supper! Supper!" to anyone who would listen.

I would already be sitting in my chair, waiting, reorganizing the food so it would all slide right by me before anyone else. Father would pray while we all organized our plates. We all gobbled down our steaming, hot food as fast we could. There was no equality of rations here. Keith took second and third helpings. The rest of us had to eat our first helpings quickly if we wanted to get more before it was all gone.

TORN

Sweat dripped feverishly down my brow as the attempt to recover the pieces took over. My body stooped down and my hands began collecting each precious piece of the original. As I worked my back ached and my fingers felt awkward. I became conscious of a slow continual shake in the muscles of my hand; I was failing. The original was scattered over the floor and I could not tell which pieces belonged where. My heart ached, it seemed the more desperate I became to fit the pieces together, the more confusing things became. Slowly I let the remaining pieces fall to the floor. I let my body crumple downward, my imagination running wild. Rocking it back and forth, I lulled myself to sleep; into a cocoon like state.

"Lost, lost," the voice whispered.

It chanted softly and sweetly, as if it were a message on of a greeting card. Lulled into a deep rest, a stillness blew down in the sound of the voice. I strained to hear the rhythm.

"Lost, lost, you are lost forever."

A sweet sensation spread over me. It was like honey dripping from a hive, saturating my skin with its sticky sweetness.

The voice returned, "Lost, lost you are lost forever."

The salty taste of sweat slid down my cheek and onto my tongue. The dream had ended. This world disappeared as quickly as it had come. I luxuriated in a moment of peace, only to begin retching uncontrollably. The stench was putrid. I jumped up only to stumble over the forgotten pieces of my memory. I had only one goal. Bursting through the bathroom door, I was already savouring the purity of the water. I needed to be clean, CLEAN, not lost.

The tap was dripping. As I twisted it, the drip turned into a torrential cleansing, a stream of living water. I ran it over my hands, my arms, and then my face. Finally, I plunged into the basin as best I could, not caring where the water splashed. The cool, wet liquid floated deliciously over my skin, then flooded into my parched soul.

My mind was repulsed at the scene I had left behind. Torn, scattered and lost, drenched in my own vomit. I would concentrate on the clarity of the water. It would bring relief. Let it spill over my skin. Let it pour into my being. The sink became too small and so I graduated to the tub. I knew the ritual, imprinted in a deep chasm of instinctual blackness; my soul, it kept me clean and kept me alive. Yes! It kept me clean and kept me alive. There was no way out. The original had disappeared before my very eyes, slowly ripped out of my hands, the jagged edges falling to my feet. Purity gone. Sweet innocence a thing of the past, dismissed with the touch of a hand. I wept silently, deserted and alone. Trying to recover the pieces was useless now. I was permanently marred. I had pushed my tormenters out of my life long ago. Yet this faint picture reappeared with a vengeance and without warning.

Dry, leathery hands moved slowly, deliberately over my body for his good pleasure, for his good pleasure. His laughter rippled in waves around me, cutting through to my soul. His words echoed on the walls of the empty room of my mind. My denial has served no good purpose. His conquest reigned in my body, robbing me of precious innocence. Tarnished, longing to be clean, in a desperate attempt, I had tried to understand this strength that ripped through choice, destroying fragile hope. I wanted nothing to do with it but had become a part of it, victimized by its power.

"There was a child went forth every day, And the first object he looked upon and received with wonder or pity or dread, that object he became, And that object became part of him for the day or a certain part of the day...or for many years or stretching cycles of years..."

Walt Whitman

THROUGH THE RINGER

Down in the dingy old basement, in the so-called bathroom, we had a dilapidated ringer washer. It agitated the clothing and it agitated Mother. It swished the clothes around in the barrel so slowly that Mother gave up all hope they would ever come out clean. But once they had been put through the ringer, they weren't so bad off.

My job was to crank the wet clothes through the archaic press. There were two rollers, squeezed close together. Mother would hold a sweater or a pair of pants close to the rollers and I would crank with all my might. Water would begin to swish swash out of the clothing, pouring back into the tub from whence it came.

At first, I could wind the lever with one hand but I would soon grow tired and have to use two. It was hard work and eventually my brow would break out into beads of sweat that dripped down my face, making it hard to see.

I sometimes had to swipe at the sweat using one of my hands, which made Mother more impatient. She was always in a hurry. She wanted to finish as quickly as possible and I was slowing her down. Eventually she would roll her eyes towards the heavens and take over my job. Then I would be the one to push the clothes through the ringers. Nevertheless, I was still too slow for Mother. I could never keep up with her frantic pace.

She held out a mental whip, urging me forward. Her entire being shouted "Faster, faster." A scowl of discontent remained planted firmly on her face.

I tried to live up to her expectations but no matter how hard I tried, it was never fast enough. I was eight and far too small for the job. I could barely reach the ringers. I should have been standing on a stool, but neither Mother nor I thought of something so simple.

Instead of having an enjoyable time working together, doing the laundry always became stressful and frustrating. My small legs grew tired and my arms ached. The production process slowed to a grinding crawl. In my Mother's eyes, this was perceived as disobedience.

I got the strap a few times for my lack of speed. The black leather belt never swayed from its intent and I never cried. I was not about to give in to this woman's bizarre requests. It confused me, spanking someone for being tired.

It was one of the many occasions that I chose to separate my soul from hers, not realizing that this behaviour only made her even more determined to conquer my being. It didn't really matter to me. I knew I could remain strong and steady despite her animosity.

This was not the end of the laundry. We had no dryer in those years so Mother would carry the laundry out to the line and I would hang it out in the wind to dry. I enjoyed this part because Mother usually went back downstairs and started another load of wash. I was left to feel the strong, sweet elements of nature on my face. I would breathe in the warm air and my tiredness would vanish.

My thoughts came alive. I was on a hot air balloon ride, and then I was a princess riding a fancy pony, then a queen ordering her servants to use the best dishes for the royal ball that night. It was refreshing not to have anyone looking over my shoulder, judging me.

The laundry was always stiff when I took it off the line. I did this even in the winter. It dried about halfway and then we brought it in to finish the process inside. It always smelled so good. The freshness of the outdoors heightened the senses and drew out the best in the cotton and polyester. It was much better than fabric softener. The outdoors just couldn't be beat.

MY DUSTY DOG

It wasn't very often you would find Mother and me sitting at the kitchen table together. But this Saturday was an exception. I was contentedly nursing my coffee and staring out the window while she opened the newspaper and began to read. This was something she did not get to do often.

We were well into our own thoughts, which was the way I preferred things, when all of a sudden, something caught her eye in the paper. Burying her head deeper into the paper, she started reading out loud. It was about a writing contest and a black standard poodle was the prize. The breeders had found an imperfection in one of their dogs. He had some white around one of his ears. I thought this was crazy and so did Mother. We discussed it at some length. We just couldn't understand how that could make a dog unfit for a show. Then again, how could we understand such breeding; all of our dogs had been Heinz 57s.

The essay was to be one page in length. That seemed extremely long to me. I never was very good at grammar and I knew the way I created sentences was awkward and disjointed. The essay had to explain why I wanted this dog and what I would do with him to train him properly.

I had to enter so I started writing the essay. I went on about how I would take good care of him; feeding him, brushing him every day. But mostly, how I would teach him tricks; jump, beg, speak, and play dead. Even if they said he was imperfect, he would be the perfect dog for me.

Now here I have to make a bit of an admission. Mother helped me out with the essay just a bit. Just between you and me, I think she wanted the dog more than I did. She became quite eloquent in her writing abilities and drew even me in with her dream of having this dog. I was sixteen so I barely snuck in the requirements for the contest. Sixteen was the cut-off age for the contest.

What felt like months went by after I mailed that very important letter. You know about time--when you are a child, everything moves intolerably slow. However, one day the phone rang, my Mother picked up the phone and I could tell by her slow smile that something was up. She handed me the phone and I heard a stranger's voice on the other end of the line. She took her jolly time in telling me I had won. She asked how school was, what my favourite subject was, she wanted to know all about me. When she finally broke the news, I was ecstatic. I don't remember exactly what I said into the phone but I do remember jumping up and down for joy inside. This was to be MY dog. I had never owned anything of my very own before.

I handed the phone back to Mother and she made all the necessary arrangements. She gave them directions to the farm and said they would be there within the week. Of course, I did not know how special this dog was. He came with papers saying he was a purebred and they said he was worth $600. He was a standard poodle, which meant he would grow to be a big dog. In the days before his arrival, I researched every encyclopedia to discover the history of poodles. He was a hunting dog, a retriever. He was very intelligent.

Finally, the day arrived. As I saw the car drive on the yard, my heart was skipping and jumping all over the place. I knew he was a puppy and would grow bigger but when I saw him, I couldn't believe how big he was. We did a little dance around each other and then I knelt on the ground beside him. He was full of kisses and his tail didn't stop wagging the whole time. He was the most beautiful dog I had ever seen. The owners handed me his papers and I took them with great excitement. They looked so official and proper. The owners stood around for quite a while chatting with Mother. Father was off somewhere fixing something. I think they were just trying to get a feel for whether this was a good place for their dog or not. They were nice people but more than anything, I wanted to start playing with my new puppy. He was as happy as could be and I could already imagine all the adventures we would have together. After the people left, everyone gathered around him to begin the process of spoiling him to death. Hugs and kisses were had by all. Personally, I believe everyone was jealous of my beautiful new dog. How couldn't they be? He was absolutely gorgeous.

Dusty was my favourite dog in the whole, wide world and I got the job of grooming him. I never really understood why I had called him Dusty until one day in early spring. It was a Saturday morning and I was relaxing with a cup of coffee. Early signs of new life were showing everywhere and I loved just looking out the kitchen window at all the creatures that were showing up. The geese on the pond were wonderfully graceful as they landed, wings spread open wide until, at the last possible second, they would glide slowly and gently onto the water. A ripple behind their graceful bodies appeared in the still water and they were down, honking wildly as if they were proud to have landed, back home once again. My eyes scanned the farmyard for other signs of life. The birds flirted with each other in the sky, the squirrels chattered to each other in the trees. Even the tender buds on the trees were whispering that the warmth of the sun was returning.

Alas, a new sight came to my eyes. There was Dusty rolling over and over again in the dirt and gravel. It was obvious to all that he was beyond itchy. Scratching himself on the dirt was the closest he could come to a measure of relief. There was a gleeful look on his face as he panted and growled in delight. I watched with great dissatisfaction. This meant that I had my real work cut out for me. I looked at my coffee cup, mostly empty, and smiled to myself. This was a sure way to get out of my household Saturday chores and enjoy nature and the outdoors. One last glance out the window and I saw that the watering hose had already been hooked up for the summer season. That was one less thing I had to worry about.

I grabbed a bucket with warm, sudsy water, the dog brush and a pair of scissors. It was time to cut away Dusty's winter coat. I jumped out the door and called his name. Dusty came running as fast as his legs would carry him. He jumped up at me, barking a friendly hello. Little did he know what was about to transpire.

I grabbed the hose and turned on the water. The temperature was colder or coldest. I held out the steady stream to my friend as a truce offering. As he lapped up the water, I grabbed a hold of his collar. This was his cue that something was up. He started out with his playful growl and then began prancing around. I sprayed the water in one quick splash across his body to get him used to the temperature with I am sure was close to -30 C.

The game was on and about to increase in its intensity. He growled and whined and I laughed. He tolerated my attempt to make something onerous into a play fight. Soon the freezing water was flying everywhere and we were both soaked to the gills. The trick, at this point, was to keep hold on his collar. If I let go for one second, I would be lost. He would be off rolling in the nasty dirt again and it would be ground into a soaked and furry dog. I literally had to drag this poodle dog up the stairs to the porch and get him to calm down before I could begin the next step.

Finally, he collapsed on the cool cement floor of the porch, lying on his side and panting from all the great fun we had just had. I took the bucket I had prepared earlier, reaching for the rag inside, and scrubbed his body with the warm water. This he loved. He lay perfectly still for me. I rubbed all the dirt and winter filth out of his skin and fur. Next came the dog brush; it was wire and heavy duty. I brushed and brushed for what seemed like an eternity. He lapped up the attention and warmed to my touch.

The sun was shining directly on him too so that helped to create some appeal in his doggy brain.

For the final step, I found the scissors sitting on the picnic table right where I had left them. I started cutting into his deep thick fur. Often I needed a second person to distract him, but this was a good day. He behaved perfectly, almost as though he knew what was expected of him. I cut and cut some more; I am sure it took at least an hour. There was black curly fur all around my mutt and me. He shed pounds in an hour--talk about a diet.

For all his perceived patience with the process when I said it was time to go he flew up and raced around and around the yard. He chased the swallows that egged him on and even flew into a rage at a squirrel that dared try to come down from his perch on the nearest tree.

OLDER AND WISER

"He who learns must suffer. And even in our sleep, pain that cannot forget falls drop by drop upon the heart, and in our own despair, against our will, comes wisdom to us by the awful grace of God."

Aeschylus

My horror had come upon me again. I was bound in the cold basement, trying not to be overcome by what was happening to me. If only my parents had been in the house, or if somehow my oppressor had left me alone!

No matter how hard I tried to be free; no matter how much I longed for another life, free from the recurring horror of his awful presence; this thing would come again. In the times of calm between attacks, I just honestly hoped that I would somehow survive. Despite the nightmares, despite my desperation for a renewed life, I still had a deep longing that something in me could stand up to what was happening.

DEEP DOWN FEELINGS

An emotional height brought on by certain causes;
A certain description using statements and clauses;
A diabolical way of creating decisions;
It's a heart, soul, will and body collision.

Copyright © 1984 Gayleen Gaeke

Addressing the inner life is unfamiliar and awkward. I was taught to believe that feelings were meant to be repressed. This was the only thing that ensured survival. Secrets must be kept, pushed down into the inner recesses of heart and mind. The cost remained high.

I have felt considerable stress over the writing of this book. I lunge towards and then away from saying something wonderful, maybe something comforting, or something incredibly influencing to the mind. I twist awkwardly forward and then back, wondering how to catch the reader's attention without sugar-coating my childhood experiences.

The description Mother, in particular, had of me as a child, is lost on me. Although personally, I believe the photographs of me to be quite striking, she made me into a devil child; evil and rotten to the core. According to her, I was a rebellious, disobedient wretch.

My art of being rebellious as a child grew out a need for self-protection against her rage and bitterness and the abuse I experienced at the hands of others in my world. But I could never tell her that. Her words of torment have come along with me on my journey. Do not get me wrong; I try to shake them, sometimes by doing good things or by performing life-changing surgery on my black heart. However, I have come to believe that a Mother's words will stick with a child for life. I have no alternative but to listen to the harsh, painful statements Mother chose to inflict upon me. With the passing of time, and with time away from

---

Somehow I got through it again. I distracted my mind from the ropes biting into my wrists, from the cold basement floor, and from what was happening to me, but I knew I would never forget my feelings of helplessness, rage, and degradation.

"Being unwanted, unloved, uncared for, forgotten by everybody, I think that is a much greater hunger, a much greater poverty than the person who has nothing to eat."

Mother Teresa

NIGHTMARES

Being dragged into the basement was another opportunity for me to detach myself from what was really happening. Those strategies worked without fail during the day, but at night the darkness crept in.

I was left vulnerable, a victim to my own body's cry for release. The nightmares overpowered my barriers, stealthily finding their way past the fortified gate of protection and into my everyday realm. They were vivid repetitions of what happened to me time and again, waking me bathed in a feverish sweat. I would recall every detail of the day's horrors.

Most nights, were filled with night terrors but when I would awake, I was usually considerably relieved to find myself safe in my bed. The flannel sheets and soft, warm blankets were a comfort. I would pull my pillow into my chest and wrap myself up in a fetal position. I would watch the light from my clock and listen to the steady click as the minutes passed by. Sometimes, I thought I saw shadows and shapes in the room. Whenever they overwhelmed me, I would close my eyes tightly, conjuring up images of "girls in white dresses and blue satin sashes, snowflakes that stayed…"

This would bring a sense of peace. The nightmare was over for another night. That thing would belong to another realm, one that I did not want to know or understand. Most times I would eventually fall back into a deep sleep.

Those times when sleep didn't come, I would wonder if the nightmare would return. My only choice then would be to lie there with my eyes closed tightly, waiting for the dawn. For sure then it would be gone for it could not stand the light.

WHISPERS

There are times in life when the subtlety is lost. Mostly, life just has a way of carrying on all on its own. It seems that it gains momentum, moving faster than ever, along with the whims of the world. We try to interject things, to bring about renewed direction and hope. Sometimes we succeed, sometimes we fail.

However, there is the very real chance that we will never come to our senses; instead, we will be carried away like a feather in the wind. We move according to our external world, not to what lives inside. Our guide becomes the clock, our actions, then reactions, people and their pleasure or displeasure. Yet none of these are identified, researched, objectified, or even spiritualized. We live our lives in denial, not admitting the source of what is driving us.

Oh, we have our crisis moments where we may face the need to change. In these moments, we cry out to life, waiting for some response to our desperate situation. We know we are not to blame for the suffering and we very much know we want the suffering to dissipate. Then why does our crying out only leave us in undeniable helplessness?

We are looking for answers within ourselves. Because we have become so shallow, we cannot see beyond our own want. Or should we call it a need? We have become so lost to our own souls we cannot reach beyond them to clearly define what is of utmost importance. In fact, we wander all around in our minds trying to access the root of the problem never really finding it. Eventually we give in to the suffering, developing an angry shell.

Protection from this confusion results in denial. We can't seem push beyond, to find that one truth that is sure to save us fro our suffering.

Suffering, whether it is given or received, appears to be the or affliction we cannot abide. Suffering brings a guilty conscienc crying out for recompense. It can bring a sense of responsibility t the abused to resolve the conflict immediately and selflessly Suffering brings a raw numbness that rises to the surface easil and is just as easily pushed down. Suffering belittles God. I causes strength of faith to rise to the surface or hopelessness tc push us deeper towards despair. Our spirituality, our core God to which we cling, is tried and tested beyond measure.

Suffering can also be unaccepted, bringing about a determination that nothing will create such a void in me again. When such barriers arise, steel armour suits itself up in the soul, causing great pain to all those around. In situations like this, the abused can become the abuser. This suffering is one of the greatest because it is completely unmanageable. When the abuser is blind, the abuse is rampant. Confrontation? Force? There is the cycle of abusing, realizing it, saying sorry, being good for a while and committing the abuse again. The victim is yanked around like a yoyo, never knowing what to believe, what is truth.

Simply put, God never meant any of this to exist. It is only because of this continual cycle of man's abuse that it continues. God's plan is for us to have internal insight, healthy communication with one another and conflict resolution. It is because He is a personal God that we can rest in His arms and trust Him that His nature is not that of man's. He did not mean for abuse to be a part of life. His love is regenerative, constant and caring. If you walk away, He walks towards you. He takes care of the helpless, giving hope, initiating love. He does not demand you move into His world. He has already moved into our world. His law is one of love. He hears suffering, listens to pain. He walks with you.

Mother, they have become less horrific; but they will always be a part of me. I must choose to fight against them.

OPENING UP TO LIFE

Looking back on this thing, this so-called life, I see that my childhood has created a multitude of scattered thoughts and feelings. Sometimes I am overwhelmed by great joy, and at other times there are scenes of incredible sorrow, causing deep depression.

I have carried this story around with me for far too long. The folder I hold is tattered and torn. Sometimes I believe that the ripped pieces of it will fall through the cracks. At other times I think that maybe it is time to drop the childhood memories to the ground, letting go of all the abuse and rage, the disappointment and fear.

Yet I cannot. I hold onto these stories of abuse as if they are what will bring wholeness. I dodge in and out of my thoughts on my childhood. The memories pull me this way and that. My complicated history is still very real to me and at times, very frightening.

On days like today I beg and plead for the memories to be gone. Yet they always show up again. They rear their ugly heads, tormenting me into thinking about the past as though it happened yesterday. I long for the day when my mind is free from their oppression. Yet I have a sinking feeling that they will only disappear bit by bit, a little each day, through the kindness of both friend and stranger. And honestly, I must learn to be kind to myself as well, patient and tolerant.

As a child, becoming invisible was the only way I knew of dealing with the abuse. That way, I did not have to dwell on the torrents of confusion and the lack of trust I felt towards certain members of my family; those who should have been my protectors. Just closing my eyes brought me to a new place. Warmth spread through my body and light shone inside; a light I could not understand, yet I needed it for survival.

Age has cracked those protective barriers and with the passage of time, my chosen strategies are now broken. Common events can act as a trigger to some blocked memory, echoing in my mind; shouting the woeful tale of secrets kept, but not forgotten. The memories that I had tucked away into small compartments have hurled themselves at me with full force.

Exposing that which was once hidden away does not happen neatly and sequentially. Bits and pieces of memory are collected from here and there. Fragments of events crack the surface of my memory, bringing with them confusion that turns to a strong ache at my core. Pain, however big or small, creates powerful panic, brought on by the thought that I will never belong. Aloneness is to be my eternal plight.

The slow and the steady admission that life has not been what I expected it to be at times has caused an even greater torment. The secrets I tried to keep sometimes tear me apart. Relinquishing control of them, giving them up, letting the memories out of their secret hiding place, has been one of the best things I have ever done. My past abuse no longer holds complete sway over my life.

Keeping those memories in the past, rather than letting them control the present, seems to be the key. I long to be free of past meetings with my old self; to be able to separate my present situation from my past abuse, seeing beyond the blurry lines of my childhood. There are moments when my longing actually becomes my reality.

In those moments, it is like a snake shedding its old skin; on the one hand joyfully free of old, itchy scales, but on the other hand, leaving it vulnerable, naked to the elements. I feel honoured that this new, white, pure cloak fits me with such warmth and closeness. But I know that this separation of past from present is not a onetime event. Like a snake, I may have to slip in and out of my bright, shiny skin many times. There are moments of feeling accepted, of feeling like I belong. But how long that feeling will last, I do not know.

Each day without an all-consuming memory is a small gift, a shiny robe, a peaceful respite. I can be alone and unafraid. Separating the memories of abuse from my present existence is like scraping off a small chunk of shedding skin once more. It is a deliverance that feels like a hot bath; it scalds but at the same time, it is soothing and potentially healing. True identity is forming.

This is what I hope for you as you read. I want this book to create hope and a longing to be released from the pain and turmoil, whatever it may be. I want you to know that it is all right to hurt. It's all right to listen to the long forgotten voice from the past, and then to speak out loud what has, for so long, been trapped inside.

LOOKING TO THE FUTURE

There are no overwhelming secrets for learning to live with Post Traumatic Stress Disorder. It can be chaotic and tiring, confusing and frightening. Growing up in a world where there was no trust or connection to others does nothing to encourage taking that first baby step of speaking secret memories out loud. There were and are many times I find myself looking for a piece of paper and pen and writing and writing until the memory is on the paper, but I may put it away to read for another day.

Connection to a real person, one that you can trust, one that you feel safe with is a huge step towards healing. I was so unaware of my own pain because of my chosen way of surviving in my given family system as a child, that expressing the abuse to someone else was exhausting. Slowly I began to trust those few safe people with my story and in return there where huge benefits. The biggest for me was being believed. This abuse was no longer a secret to be kept, pushed down, but a very real part of my life.

Hearing someone say, "I believe you and in you," was and is very powerful.

The unfortunate part for me was that the more I was believed the more I remembered. At times it took me back to my childhood and I learnt quickly that working through traumatic events is messy and sometimes feels hopeless. Re-living again and again each night, waking up in panic with gruesome images left in my mind, starting out in my bed at night and waking up somewhere else, this was and is all very real and terrifying. The need to have someone to calm me and bring me back to the present was crucial to my healing. I have no doubt these events may follow me throughout life. Managing them and putting coping strategies in place is no small task and cannot be done alone. Learning to ask for help in my life has been very healing. It has given me a hope that as I continue to travel this journey, I will have a deeper understanding of what I am travelling through.

Healing with my older brother has been a roller coaster of sorts. There is never just one perspective in life, and by talking with him, the beginning of healing came about. At first we were careful with each other, maybe not saying too much, but eventually we shared experiences which at times added to the confusion and at other times clarified them. Forgiveness is not a snap of the finger.

Being left with trauma in mind and body creating havoc in my life reminds me almost daily of the abuse of my assailants and my disjointed family system. Letting go of the past doesn't just mean throwing it up into the sky, sometimes it means slogging through painful memories, and reaching for a new depth of understanding. Coming out on the other side, brings a new self to know and understand. Choice is all there is, strength of will can bring moments of true joy. Conquering comes as a part of the process, not the end result.

Clinging to those moments of true connection with self and others brings a semblance of calm to a traumatic world. I cherish

Somehow I got through it again. I distracted my mind from the ropes biting into my wrists, from the cold basement floor, and from what was happening to me, but I knew I would never forget my feelings of helplessness, rage, and degradation.

"Being unwanted, unloved, uncared for, forgotten by everybody, I think that is a much greater hunger, a much greater poverty than the person who has nothing to eat."

Mother Teresa

NIGHTMARES

Being dragged into the basement was another opportunity for me to detach myself from what was really happening. Those strategies worked without fail during the day, but at night the darkness crept in.

I was left vulnerable, a victim to my own body's cry for release. The nightmares overpowered my barriers, stealthily finding their way past the fortified gate of protection and into my everyday realm. They were vivid repetitions of what happened to me time and again, waking me bathed in a feverish sweat. I would recall every detail of the day's horrors.

Most nights, were filled with night terrors but when I would awake, I was usually considerably relieved to find myself safe in my bed. The flannel sheets and soft, warm blankets were a comfort. I would pull my pillow into my chest and wrap myself up in a fetal position. I would watch the light from my clock and listen to the steady click as the minutes passed by. Sometimes, I thought I saw shadows and shapes in the room. Whenever they overwhelmed me, I would close my eyes tightly, conjuring up images of "girls in white dresses and blue satin sashes, snowflakes that stayed..."

This would bring a sense of peace. The nightmare was over for another night. That thing would belong to another realm, one that I did not want to know or understand. Most times I would eventually fall back into a deep sleep.

Those times when sleep didn't come, I would wonder if the nightmare would return. My only choice then would be to lie there with my eyes closed tightly, waiting for the dawn. For sure then it would be gone for it could not stand the light.

WHISPERS

There are times in life when the subtlety is lost. Mostly, life just has a way of carrying on all on its own. It seems that it gains momentum, moving faster than ever, along with the whims of the world. We try to interject things, to bring about renewed direction and hope. Sometimes we succeed, sometimes we fail.

However, there is the very real chance that we will never come to our senses; instead, we will be carried away like a feather in the wind. We move according to our external world, not to what lives inside. Our guide becomes the clock, our actions, then reactions, people and their pleasure or displeasure. Yet none of these are identified, researched, objectified, or even spiritualized. We live our lives in denial, not admitting the source of what is driving us.

Oh, we have our crisis moments where we may face the need to change. In these moments, we cry out to life, waiting for some response to our desperate situation. We know we are not to blame for the suffering and we very much know we want the suffering to dissipate. Then why does our crying out only leave us in undeniable helplessness?

We are looking for answers within ourselves. Because we have become so shallow, we cannot see beyond our own want. Or should we call it a need? We have become so lost to our own souls we cannot reach beyond them to clearly define what is of utmost importance. In fact, we wander all around in our minds trying to access the root of the problem never really finding it. Eventually we give in to the suffering, developing an angry shell.

Protection from this confusion results in denial. We can't seem to push beyond, to find that one truth that is sure to save us from our suffering.

Suffering, whether it is given or received, appears to be the one affliction we cannot abide. Suffering brings a guilty conscience crying out for recompense. It can bring a sense of responsibility to the abused to resolve the conflict immediately and selflessly. Suffering brings a raw numbness that rises to the surface easily and is just as easily pushed down. Suffering belittles God. It causes strength of faith to rise to the surface or hopelessness to push us deeper towards despair. Our spirituality, our core God to which we cling, is tried and tested beyond measure.

Suffering can also be unaccepted, bringing about a determination that nothing will create such a void in me again. When such barriers arise, steel armour suits itself up in the soul, causing great pain to all those around. In situations like this, the abused can become the abuser. This suffering is one of the greatest because it is completely unmanageable. When the abuser is blind, the abuse is rampant. Confrontation? Force? There is the cycle of abusing, realizing it, saying sorry, being good for a while and committing the abuse again. The victim is yanked around like a yoyo, never knowing what to believe, what is truth.

Simply put, God never meant any of this to exist. It is only because of this continual cycle of man's abuse that it continues. God's plan is for us to have internal insight, healthy communication with one another and conflict resolution. It is because He is a personal God that we can rest in His arms and trust Him that His nature is not that of man's. He did not mean for abuse to be a part of life. His love is regenerative, constant and caring. If you walk away, He walks towards you. He takes care of the helpless, giving hope, initiating love. He does not demand you move into His world. He has already moved into our world. His law is one of love. He hears suffering, listens to pain. He walks with you.

Copyright © 1997 Gayleen Gaeke

DEEP DOWN FEELINGS

An emotional height brought on by certain causes;
A certain description using statements and clauses;
A diabolical way of creating decisions;
It's a heart, soul, will and body collision.

Copyright © 1984 Gayleen Gaeke

Addressing the inner life is unfamiliar and awkward. I was taught to believe that feelings were meant to be repressed. This was the only thing that ensured survival. Secrets must be kept, pushed down into the inner recesses of heart and mind. The cost remained high.

I have felt considerable stress over the writing of this book. I lunge towards and then away from saying something wonderful, maybe something comforting, or something incredibly influencing to the mind. I twist awkwardly forward and then back, wondering how to catch the reader's attention without sugar-coating my childhood experiences.

The description Mother, in particular, had of me as a child, is lost on me. Although personally, I believe the photographs of me to be quite striking, she made me into a devil child; evil and rotten to the core. According to her, I was a rebellious, disobedient wretch.

My art of being rebellious as a child grew out a need for self-protection against her rage and bitterness and the abuse I experienced at the hands of others in my world. But I could never tell her that. Her words of torment have come along with me on my journey. Do not get me wrong; I try to shake them, sometimes by doing good things or by performing life-changing surgery on my black heart. However, I have come to believe that a Mother's words will stick with a child for life. I have no alternative but to listen to the harsh, painful statements Mother chose to inflict upon me. With the passing of time, and with time away from